WALKING AS JESUS WALKED

WALKING AS JESUS WALKED

MAKING DISCIPLES THE WAY JESUS DID

DANN SPADER

MOODY PUBLISHERS

CHICAGO

All Scripture quotations, unless otherwise indicated, are taken from the *Holy Bible, New International Version*®, NIV®. Copyright ©1973, 1978, 1984 by Biblica, Inc.™ Used by permission of Zondervan. All rights reserved worldwide. www.zondervan.com

Scripture quotations marked NCV are from the *Holy Bible, New Century Version*, copyright © 1987, 1988, 1991 by Word Publishing, Nashville, TN 37214. Used by permission.

Scripture quotations marked NLT are taken from the *Holy Bible, New Living Translation*, copyright © 1996, 2004. Used by permission of Tyndale House Publishers, Inc., Wheaton, Illinois 60189, U.S.A. All rights reserved.

Scripture quotations marked NASB are taken from the *New American Standard Bible*®, Copyright © 1960, 1962, 1963, 1968, 1971, 1972, 1973, 1975, 1977, 1995 by The Lockman Foundation. Used by permission. www.Lockman.org.

Scripture quotations marked NKJV are taken from the *New King James Version*. Copyright © 1982 by Thomas Nelson, Inc. Used by permission. All rights reserved.

All emphasis in Scripture has been added by the author.

Edited by Pam Pugh
Interior Design: Smartt Guys design
Cover Design: Kathryn Joachim
Cover and Interior Images: Albert Smirnov, iStockphoto.com, #12478206,
　　　　　　　　iStockphoto.com #2118236,#2192892, #10638727, #15874634

Library of Congress Catologing-in-Publication Data

Spader, Dann.
　Walking as Jesus walked : making disciples the way Jesus did / Dann Spader.
　　p. cm.
　Includes bibliographical references.
　ISBN 978-0-8024-4709-8
　1. Jesus Christ--Example. 2. Discipling (Christianity) I.Title.
　BT304.2.S63 2011
　232--dc22

　　　　　　　　　　　　　　2011013774

We hope you enjoy this book from Moody Publishers. Our goal is to provide high-quality, thought-provoking books and products that connect truth to your real needs and challenges. For more information on other books and products written and produced from a biblical perspective, go to www.moodypublishers.com or write to:

Moody Publishers
820 N. LaSalle Boulevard
Chicago, IL 60610

9 10 8

Printed in the United States of America

To my wife, Char, my best friend and partner for over thirty years,
to our three wonderful daughters . . . Julie, Jamie, and Christy,
to our two sons-in-law . . . Pete and Brandon,
and to Keira and Elyse, two of the cutest granddaughters anyone could ever have!
Thanks for making our family such a wonderful part of life!

and

To my executive Bible study guys . . . you truly are a band of brothers.
Your passion for the Lord and heart to see His kingdom advanced is inspirational.
Thanks for your friendship and encouragement.
Special thanks to Brian Campbell, Bob Chicoine, Scott Kirk, Bob Spence, and Gary
Vargyas for your time and input in helping make this a better Bible study tool.
And special thanks also to Barry, our "seeker" friend,
who gave us special insight into this study as only someone
who is still "kicking the tires and checking out Christianity" could.
I can't wait until the day you make the decision to
accept Christ as your Savior. We all love you!

EXPLORE MORE ONLINE

WEEK 1 WEEK 2 WEEK 3

Watch Dann introduce each week at **WalkingAsJesus.com**

MOODY PUBLISHERS

CONTENTS

HOW TO GET THE MOST FROM THIS STUDY

Walking as Jesus Walked is a resource for small groups or individuals who have a desire to study the life of Christ and go deeper in understanding what the Scriptures mean in 1 John 2:6 when it says, "Whoever claims to live in Him must walk as Jesus did." This resource has been developed as a 10–12 week study, but can be adapted to a longer time frame, depending on the needs and interests of the group.

Designed primarily as a small group interactive study, this resource can also be used for personal study at your own pace. With interesting questions for individual preparation, group discussion and interaction will aid in going deeper in this material. Feel free to use it as best serves your needs or that of your group. A leader's guide, along with a personal video from the author introducing each lesson, is available online at WalkingAsJesus.com. These videos and leader's guides are free resources and can be used in any way that will serve your group.

Each session in this book has been designed with an introductory overview called "Getting Started" followed by five "Days" of personal study to be done prior to the group meeting (or six when you take a day for the overview). Each of these "Days" takes approximately 10–15 minutes to complete. Feel free to mark up your book, adding additional insights or questions you may have as you study the text. Bring any of these questions or insights with you to the small group interaction time. The free online leader's guide will serve as a tool to help the group facilitator guide the group interaction time.

At the end of each lesson is a supplemental "For deeper reflection" designed to provide ongoing questions for further thought. You may want to use some of these questions for group interaction. They are also designed to take the lesson to a deeper level.

Our prayer is that you will gain a fresh look at Christ and see in His humanity a model of how God intended us to live life. Allow the Spirit of God to teach you . . . look honestly at the Scriptures . . . and allow Him to transform your life. Hebrews 3:1 in *The Message* version of the Bible challenges us "to take a good hard look at Jesus. He's the centerpiece of everything we believe." For over thirty-five years I have been studying the life of Christ . . . and what I love about Him is that He is a very deep well . . . continually giving us new living insights about living for Him. Our desire in writing this study was to help you "take a good hard look at Jesus."

WALKING AS JESUS WALKED

See WalkingAsJesus.com for video resources specific to this week's study.

GETTING STARTED

Max Lucado begins his excellent book *Just Like Jesus* with this powerful challenge:

What if, for one day, Jesus were to become you?

What if, for twenty-four hours, Jesus wakes up in your bed, walks in your shoes, lives in your house, assumes your schedule? Your boss becomes his boss, your mother becomes his mother, your pains become his pains? With one exception, nothing about your life changes. Your health doesn't change. Your circumstances don't change. Your schedule isn't altered. Your problems aren't solved. Only one change occurs.

What if, for one day and one night, Jesus lives your life with his heart? Your heart gets the day off, and your life is led by the heart of Christ. His priorities govern your actions. His passions drive your decisions. His love directs your behavior.[1]

What would you be like?

Max goes on to talk about the "heart" of Jesus that can be ours—a heart of forgiveness, compassion, purity, worship, and hope. This is a valuable exercise, for it gives us an opportunity to reflect on how our lives might change if we truly allow Jesus to renew our heart and mind. It takes seriously the challenge of Philippians 2:5, that we should "have the same mindset [i.e., 'heart'] as Christ Jesus."

But is it enough to *think* like Jesus? The New Century Version (NCV) translates Philippians 2:5 a little differently. There Paul commands his readers to "think *and act* like Christ Jesus." In other words, Paul's command is not just that we learn to think like Jesus but also that we learn to behave like Jesus. What a challenge!

Great as it is, this challenge is at the heart of this study. We want to look not just at the heart of Jesus but also at His habits, commitments, and behaviors. We want to probe deep and ask the difficult why and how questions about Jesus' actions: How did He nurture His relationship with the Father? Why did He pray? How did He learn obedience? Why was the Holy Spirit so critical in His walk?

In this study, we will seek to answer these questions by taking a close and focused look at Christ's life. We will spend the majority of our time, though not all of it, in the Gospels, since the Gospel writers in particular sought to portray for the rest of us how Jesus lived His life. But the challenge to think and act like Jesus is not only found in the Gospels. In 1 John 2:6 we find the challenge of Philippians 2:5 stated in a different way. This is the verse from which the title of our study is taken.

Open your Bible, take a close look at 1 John 2:6, and copy it below. Highlight what you feel are the two or three most important words.

Whoever (claims) to live in him must (live) as Jesus (did)

What words did you choose? Why?

Claim - believe ∴ live

This study is designed to help us discover not only *what* Jesus did, but also *how* Jesus did what He did. We want to pause long enough to evaluate what Jesus may have been thinking when He behaved in certain ways. As we examine why Jesus acted the way He did, we will be looking for a pattern—a pattern we can follow in order to faithfully think and act as He did.

My prayer is that you'll catch a fresh glimpse of the biblical Jesus in the coming weeks. As you go through this study, I encourage you to evaluate any stereotypes you may have of the Jesus who lived two thousand years ago. Hold them up to the light of Scripture and see if the images match up. My prayer is that you will find the Jesus who is alive today and still calls us to follow Him. Jesus is alive, relevant, and challenging. He always gives us new insights and He challenges many of our basic life assumptions. He desires for us to continually increase in our love and understanding of Him. May this study help you gain a deeper respect for the real Jesus of the Scriptures . . . and be ever eager to always "walk as Jesus walked."

What it does not mean

Before we begin, it will be helpful to discuss what the command in 1 John 2:6 to "walk as Jesus walked" does and does not mean.

As much as I hate to admit it, 1 John 2:6 does not mean that we are to move to Israel and walk where Jesus literally walked. I love Israel and have often longed to walk the famous "Jesus Path," the path mapped out for tourists there. The Jesus Path lets you walk *where* Jesus walked. But it doesn't help you walk *as* Jesus walked.

Walking as Jesus walked also does not mean that we are to buy a robe and some good leather sandals, grow our hair long, and walk from town to town. While this might make a good movie (or at least provide entertainment for our neighbors), it does not fulfill the command of 1 John 2:6.

What it does mean

How then, in the 21st century, are we to obey this command? What does it look like to walk as Jesus walked?

The word translated "walk" in this passage is the Greek word *peripateo*. It is used in the New Testament to mean "following, making progress, regulating one's life, or conducting oneself" after the pattern of another person. To walk like Jesus, then, means that we are to emulate the pattern of living that Jesus modeled for us.

What is your initial impression of what this means to walk as Jesus walked? Describe it as clearly as you can below:

> Slow down, live in the moment, to be able to do devotions and learn how to walk as Jesus walked.

FOR DEEPER REFLECTION

Look closely at the context of 1 John 2:1–10. Read it aloud. What do you think was on John's mind when he commanded us to walk as Jesus walked?

In what ways do you think it's possible to walk as Jesus walked?

In what areas do you think it's impossible to walk as Jesus walked?

The Message of Jesus DAY 1

As I have studied the life of Christ over the last thirty-five years, I have concluded that there are at least three approaches to the subject. The first approach is to study His message. What did He say? What did He mean? The people who heard Jesus' message recognized that He came with a new teaching, and He delivered it with unparalleled authority (Mark 1:27).

Moreover, Jesus articulated His message in a variety of ways and in a variety of settings. He delivered sermons, spoke in parables, and used illustrations from daily life. As a result, His message was both simple and profound at the same time. His message of the good news of the kingdom was radical in its impact and scope. It touched every area of life. It was filled with hope and expectation. It challenged the basic worldviews—both Jewish and Roman—of His day. A person could spend his or her entire life (and eternity!) studying Christ's message and probably never fully grasp all that He had to say.

Over the next couple of days, we'll look at two other approaches to the study of Jesus' life. Today, we'll start our investigation by looking at His message.

Look up these verses and write down what they tell us about the everyday message Jesus communicated:

Matthew 4:17

Repent, for the Kingdom of heaven has come.

Matthew 6:19

Do not store up treasures on earth that could be destroyed.

> I am an historian, I am not a believer, but I must confess as a historian that this penniless preacher from Nazareth is irrevocably the very center of history. Jesus Christ is easily the most dominant figure in all history.
>
> —H. G. Wells

Matthew 6:31–33

Do not worry about what you should eat drink, or wear. Seek Christ's kingdom + his righteousness. All these things will be given to you.

Matthew 9:12–13

We are to give mercy to the sick, the sinners, the least of these.

Matthew 10:37–39

Love God first before anyone else. We are to take up our cross whole-heartedly. Wrap our whole life in Christ.

Mark 10:45

We are to serve others.

Luke 5:12–13

We are to have faith that God can do amazing things in our lives.

How did those closest to Jesus respond to His message?

Matthew 7:28–29

They were amazed because he did not teach as one in authority.

Matthew 13:54–56

They were amazed because he was born pe ordinary parents.

FOR DEEPER REFLECTION

Identify some of the key themes in Jesus' teaching. What seems to come up again and again?

Do not dwell or worry about earthly things. Have faith in God.

What is missing from Jesus' teaching that you expected to find there? That is, what doesn't He talk about?

How would you summarize the message of Jesus?

This world is not our forever home. Focus on the eternal and have faith, hope, + trust in God.

DAY 2 The Methods of Jesus

Last time we examined the message of Jesus. There is another common approach to the study of the life of Christ. Rather than emphasize the message of Jesus, some people look at His *methods*.

In his classic book *The Master Plan of Evangelism*, Robert Coleman examined Jesus' strategy for spreading His message about the kingdom in the world. Focusing on the methods of Jesus requires asking a new set of questions: How did Jesus share His message? How did He identify, train, and send His disciples? What were the strategies that motivated His decisions?

Focusing on Jesus' methods doesn't mean we neglect His message. To the contrary, this is a different look at Jesus that gives us brand-new insight into His message. When we begin to see and apply Christ's methods to the pattern of our own life, we gain a fresh and powerful new understanding of Jesus. Christ's methods help us appreciate and understand His message, for Jesus' methods were as unique and powerful as the message He taught.

Today we want to look briefly at some of the methods of Jesus. But before we begin, what would you list as some of His unique methods? List as many as you possibly can.

Telling stories to illustrate a lesson. Object lessons. Loving, compassionate actions.

Look at these passages of Scripture and identify what they tell us about some of the methods Jesus used.

John 1:14 (Hint: What was Jesus' method of choosing to interact with us?)

He dwelt with people. He visited and sat with people.

John 1:37–39 (Hint: How did Jesus relate to His first followers?)

He invited his followers to come with him.

John 2:1–3 (Hint: Where did Jesus choose to do His first miracle? Why do you think He made this choice?)

At a wedding. A ceremony of love. Jesus was all about love.

John 2:13–19 (Hint: How did Jesus act during His first public Passover?)

He spoke & acted with authority when needed.

John 3:22 (Hint: What was Jesus' main priority?)

Spending time with his disciples and baptizing them.

John 4:1–4 (Hint: What did Jesus avoid? What didn't He avoid?)

Jesus did not avoid confrontation.

John 7:1 (Hint: What was Jesus intentional about at this stage of His ministry?)

Staying alive. Not creating more dissension.

John 8:49–59 (Hint: How subtle was Jesus in His dealings with Jewish leaders?)

In hindsight the Jewish leaders might have realized that Jesus was telling the truth. They chose not to understand so they had closed ears.

John 13:1, 4–5 (Hint: How did Jesus deal with His disciples?)

He loved his disciples and served them.

Matthew 11:29–30 versus/contrasted with Matthew 23:13–17 (Hint: How does Jesus' tone differ between needy sinners and arrogant Pharisees?)

He is calm - calming with the needy sinners. He is in the faces of the arrogant Pharisees.

FOR DEEPER REFLECTION

What method(s) of Jesus do you feel were the most radical?

I think the audience determines the method. All are radical.

Which method(s) do you feel are missing in some ministries today?

Which method(s) of Jesus do you need to develop in your own life? Why?

The Model of Jesus DAY 3

For the past couple of days, we've explored the message and methods of Jesus. If we want to walk as Jesus walked, it is critical that we understand what He taught and how He lived. However, for many, a focus only on the message of Jesus can result in a *message-centered* Christianity. Are we talking right? Are saying the right things? Is the preacher preaching the right things? With this mind-set, being a Christian becomes mainly about getting the *message* correct—saying the right things.

A focus on only the methods of Jesus can, in the same way, end up in a *method-centered* Christianity. Are we acting right? Are we doing the right things? Are our leaders acting the right way? Being a Christian becomes mainly about doing things right.

Nevertheless, the Scriptures point us beyond both the message and methods of Jesus and challenge us to look at the very *model* of His life. After all, we are commanded to walk "as" Jesus walked. To do this, we need to look at the complete pattern of His life and pattern our life after His.

This approach requires new questions: What was Jesus like in His humanity? How did Jesus behave as a real man in a real time and place?

When we focus on Jesus' message and methods we are considering His deity—what was He saying? And how, as God incarnate, was He acting?

But looking at the model of Jesus' life is more about who Jesus was as a human being. The pattern of Jesus' life is the example of what it means to be fully human. This is the heart of the challenge of 1 John 2:6. When Jesus became flesh and dwelt among us, He told us to look hard at how He lived His life and to follow that pattern. The operative word in 1 John 2:6 becomes the little word "as." Looking close at Christ in His humanity causes us to look at our humanity and to examine it in light of Jesus' example. Walking as Jesus walked becomes our focus.

> As a child I received instruction both in the Bible and in the Talmud. I am a Jew, but I am enthralled by the luminous figure of the Nazarene. No one can read the Gospels without feeling the actual presence of Jesus. His personality pulsates in every word. No myth is filled with such life.
>
> —Albert Einstein

As was noted before, Philippians 2:5 (NCV) says that we are to "think and act like Jesus." How does this verse challenge us to look beyond the message and methods of Jesus?

We should understand how Jesus acted even when he wasn't preaching.

Read the following passages. How do they challenge us to look beyond Jesus' message and method, and call us to imitate the very example of His life?

John 6:57

Jesus wants himself to be part of every area of our lives,

John 13:15

Jesus is our example, we should do as he did.

John 13:34

We are to love one another like Jesus did.

John 14:12

If we believe in Jesus then we will be able to do great things like he did.

John 15:10

Obey his commands and we will remain in his love.

John 17:18 and 20:21 *sanctify – set apart*
We are to be sent and
set apart from the
world.

1 Peter 2:21

Christ suffered and sometimes
we need to suffer but we can
rest assured that Christ is
with us.

1 John 2:6

If we claim to living him
we must live as Jesus did.

FOR DEEPER REFLECTION

Which of the above statements do you find most challenging? Why?

1 Peter 2:21. No one wants
to suffer.

Do you find it hard to believe that you could think and act like Jesus? Explain your answer.

I don't find it hard to believe
but hard to do.

If you study only the message or methods of Jesus, is it possible to miss the true meaning of His life?
How?

No

DAY 4 A Summary of Jesus' Life

The gospel of Matthew provides two famous statements that summarize His life and mission for His disciples. The first is known as the Great Commandment, the other the Great Commission.

The Great Commandment is found in Matthew 22:37–40. What is at the central challenge of this commandment? How does this commandment go beyond Christ's message and methods?

> Love your your God with your
> entire being and love your
> neighbor. If Christ did not
> give his message + methods in lov
> they would not been void

Some have described this commandment as simply loving God and loving people. It identifies the heart motive of Jesus and a fulfillment of the laws of the Old Testament. This is the motive behind the mission. If love for God and love for people were at the very core of Christ's life here on earth, what are the immediate implications for us today?

> We are to do the same in our
> message + methods.

The Great Commission is found in at least five passages of Scripture (Matthew 28:16–20, Mark 16:14–18, Luke 24:44–49, John 20:19–23, and Acts 1:4–8), but the most common is Matthew 28:16–20. How would you summarize the Great Commission?

> Go and share God's love by
> making disciples and sharing
> God's message + methods trough
> the power of the Holy Spirit.

Matthew 28 contains three verbs—*go, baptize,* and *teach to obey* that modify the command to "make disciples." This command literally means to make disciples who can make disciples. This is to be done in all nations. Many scholars believe Jesus gave this commission to the five hundred spoken about in 1 Corinthians 15:6. Regardless of whom it was directed to, it serves as a summary of Jesus' life and a call to Jesus' followers to do what He did: make disciples who can make disciples and do this to the ends of the earth. While this commission is great in terms of its challenge and scope, it really is an everyday commission. It is for every believer, every moment of their everyday life. After all, Jesus promised, "I am with you always [this literally means the whole of every moment], even to the end of the age."

If you summarize the motive and the mission of Jesus as simply loving God and loving people (Great Commandment) by making disciples who can make disciples (Great Commission), what does this tell us about the focus of Christ's life? What effect should this have on our daily life?

Love, love, love,
Love everybody always. Bob Goff

Interestingly enough is that in this text there is a second command at the end of Matthew 28:20. The command is the simple Greek work *idou,* translated in the NIV as simply "And surely" or in some translations as "Behold." This literally means that while we are fulfilling the command to make disciples, we are to keep our eyes on Jesus because He said, "surely I am with you always, to the very end of the age."

Could it be that the degree to which we keep our eyes on Jesus, walking as He walked, is the degree to which we will be able to fulfill this everyday commission and everyday commandment?

As we continue in this study, you will see I passionately believe that we are to go beyond just the message of Jesus, and even the methods of Jesus, and dive deep into the very model of His life. We are to "think and act like Jesus" (Philippians 2:5 NCV). The very Jesus, who walked on this earth as the perfect human, set an example for us to follow. Jesus began and ended the gospel of John with the phrase "follow Me," and He meant it (John 1:43; 21:22). As we continue in this study, we will seek to unpack what this calling looks like.

FOR DEEPER REFLECTION

Look carefully at the Great Commandment in Matthew 22:15–40. Read it aloud. What is the context and background of these verses?

How can a message or lifestyle of "love" often silence the arguments of your critics? Give an example from personal experience.

How does "making disciples who can make disciples" differ from just "making disciples"? Give an illustration of when you've seen this lived out.

"Follow Me" DAY 5

The mandate for every Christian is clear. We are to follow Jesus. As we stated last time, this is clear in the bookends of John's gospel where Jesus says, "Follow me" (John 1:43; 21:22).

The Greek word translated "follow Me" in John 1:43 and 21:22 is *akoloutheow*, which means, "to walk in the steps of, to conform to, or to follow behind closely." Growing up on a farm in South Dakota, I would often wake up early with my dad to go out to the barn and do chores. I remember my father leading the way on more than one occasion through a winter snowstorm, cutting a path in the snow with his strong legs. I simply followed in his path. This is the image Jesus' words "follow Me" bring to my mind. *I am the author and perfecter of your faith*, Jesus says. *I have gone before and blazed a trail for you. Now walk in My steps.*

The concept is clear. But it poses a radical challenge. How do we truly follow Jesus today? What does this command mean in the 21st century? How do we walk as Jesus walked?

The key to really following Jesus is making sure we are following the real Jesus!

The Scriptures testify to at least three different periods in Jesus' existence: the preincarnate Christ, the incarnate Christ, and the resurrected Christ. The preincarnate Christ played a key role in creation.

What do you discover about the preincarnate Christ in these verses?

John 1:1–4

He was with God in the beginning.
Through him all things were made.
In him was life. Life was light.

John 8:58

He was before Abraham.

> People talk about imitating Christ, and imitate Him in the little trifling formal things, such as washing the feet, saying His prayer, and so on; but if anyone attempts the real imitation of Him, there are no bounds to the outcry with which the presumption of that person is condemned.
>
> —Florence Nightingale

John 17:5

Jesus was in God's Presence and Jesus found glory from God.

Colossians 1:15–17

Jesus is the image of God. Through him all things were created. and for him.

Hebrews 1:3, 10

Jesus is the radiance of God. Exact representation of God. Sat at the right hand of God Jesus laid the foundations of earth. Earth is the works of his hands.

After His earthly ministry and resurrection, this God/Man Jesus ascended into heaven. Having become flesh and dwelt among us, Jesus is now the firstborn from among the dead (Colossians 1:18). The resurrected Christ now has a unique role.

Read the following passages. What can we learn about Christ's present role as the resurrected Christ?

John 14:18–20

Jesus is Present. We don't see him. We live through him.

John 14:23

He loves us.

Romans 8:34

Intercedes for us.

Ephesians 4:7–11

He gave us all spiritual gifts.

Colossians 1:18

He is the head of the church.
He has supremacy.

Ephesians 1:20–23

He has dominion over
everything.

Hebrews 13:20–21

Shepherd of the sheep. Equips
us with everything good for doing
his will. Works in us what is pleasing
to him.

It is important to understand that we are not called to walk as the preincarnate Christ or the resurrected Christ. We are called to walk as Jesus walked when He became flesh and dwelt among us. The fully human Christ modeled for us what true, biblical humanity should look like. The pattern of the incarnate Christ is the one we are called to follow.

I have seen many people shrink from the challenge of walking as Jesus walked, because they believe several false claims, including:

1. Jesus was God, but I am just a human being; therefore I could never do what He did!
2. Jesus was sinless, but I am sinful; therefore I cannot do what Jesus did.

3. Jesus was a superhuman, but I am just an average person; therefore I cannot do what He did.

Each of these views has some truth in it. Unfortunately, they are all based on some false assumptions that have serious consequences. Understanding the true humanity of Jesus will give us confidence that we can truly walk as Jesus walked.

In the rest of this study, we will look more in depth at Christ's humanity and its implications for us as we walk as Jesus walked.

FOR DEEPER REFLECTION

Referencing the above passages in your Bible, describe how these two roles of Jesus—preincarnate and resurrected—differ.

Preincarnate - He was present with God only.
Resurrected - He is present with God + us. He works on our behalf.

How are they similar?

He does the work of God.

What have you found the most challenging in Week 1?

What was something new that you realized?

WEEK 1 SUMMARY

Jesus is our model for life and ministry, and we are commanded to "walk as He walked."

HOW REAL IS YOUR JESUS?

See WalkingAsJesus.com for video resources specific to this week's study.

GETTING STARTED

Many people struggle with walking as Jesus walked because they have concluded that since Jesus was God and we are not, we can't do what Jesus did. If this is the case, then Jesus was unrealistic to tell us to walk as He walked even though He knew we could never do it. If we cannot do what Jesus did, then we are faced with a real dilemma, since Jesus Himself commanded us to follow His example.

In order to resolve this dilemma we must look closely at the humanity of Jesus. I need to ask a tough question: "How real is your Jesus?" Are you trying to follow the real Jesus? Or are you trying to follow a superhuman Jesus that is a figment of the modern mind?

We come by our view of Jesus as a superman honestly. By the middle of the nineteenth century, theological liberalism was sweeping Europe. Liberal theologians began to champion the humanity of Jesus because it was a way to ignore and downplay Christ's deity.[1] In response, conservative theologians began to emphasize Christ's deity, making belief in the divinity of Jesus a litmus test for true Christian orthodoxy—and rightly so.

Unfortunately, the pendulum has swung so far in the process that few of us ever stop to think about the profound implications of Jesus' humanity. To properly understand the command to walk as Jesus walked, we must develop a correct understanding of both His deity and His humanity.

Let us begin our investigation by considering the following questions.

Was Jesus fully God? Read what Paul says in Colossians 2:9.

All the fullness of the Deity (God) lives in bodily form.

Not only was Jesus fully God, but He was also fully human. What light does Hebrews 2:14–18 shed on this?

Jesus had flesh + blood. Fully human in every way.

Okay. It is easy to *say* that Jesus is both fully God and fully human. But what does it mean? Being fully God and fully human creates serious difficulties for anyone trying to imagine how this could work. For example, God is present everywhere (omnipresent), yet when He walked on this earth, Jesus was not. Each morning He woke up and set priorities for the day. He made decisions regarding the most strategic way to make His life count. Since, in His humanity, Jesus could not be everywhere at the same time, He faced choices, just as we do. He had to choose where to go and where not to go, whom to talk with and whom to avoid. He was not omnipresent in His humanity. So how does this work . . . fully God and fully man at the same time? Can you feel the tension building?

Furthermore, God is all-knowing (omniscient), yet there were things that Jesus, in His humanity, did not know. (We will discuss in future sessions times when Jesus does know in His spirit what people are thinking.) He did not know His cousin John the Baptist had died until someone told Him (Matthew 14:13). He did not know the time of His own return (Matthew 24:36). How could Jesus, as God, know all things, but, in His humanity, not know all things?

There are more challenges still. God is all-powerful (omnipotent), yet Jesus in His humanity "could not do any miracles there" (Mark 6:5). His power was seemingly limited by the people's lack of faith. How could Jesus, as God, be all-powerful while, in His humanity, He was not?

The answers to these questions are a mystery that has caused many to stumble. As Charles Ryrie has said, "every major heresy has stemmed from a faulty understanding of 'fully God' and 'fully man.'"[2] As difficult as this is to understand, it is crucial. We know that Jesus had to be fully human for our salvation to be fully complete. This is the message of Hebrews 2 (see especially 2:17). We also know that Jesus was fully God by the claims that He made. How can this be? Or as Augustine said, "If you diminish His humanity, then you diminish what He did for us. If you make Him less than human, then our salvation is less than complete."

The answer can be summarized this way: *In eternity past, Jesus made the decision, that when He walked here on earth, He would veil His deity so that His humanity could be fully expressed.*

Other theologians have expressed the matter in the following ways:

"Never less than God, Jesus chose to live His life, never more than man."[3]

"His deity was unexpressed, so that His humanity could be fully expressed."[4]

"Jesus refused to rely on His deity to make obedience easier for Him."[5]

Consider this illustration. If you have a credit card, you know it has an account number, an expiration date, and a credit limit. Imagine that Jesus carried the ultimate Master's Card, the *God card*. The account number was a perfect *7777 7777 7777 7777*. The expiration date was eternity. And, of course, His credit limit was infinite since Jesus created and owns the whole world. Jesus had the God card. He carried the God card. He was, at His very core, God.

Here's the point: while Jesus walked on earth, He did not use the God card!

> There was no identity crisis in the life of Jesus Christ. He knew who He was. He knew where He had come from, and why He was here. And He knew where He was going. And when you are that liberated, then you can serve.
>
> **—Howard Hendricks**

That's how He lived a fully human life. Satan's initial strategy in the wilderness was to try to get Jesus to use His God card. Satan attempted to get Jesus to take shortcuts to glory . . . "If you are the Son of God . . ." was the challenge (Matthew 4:3, 6). If Satan could have tempted Jesus into using His God card, then He would not have "been like His brothers [us] in every way" (Hebrews 2:17). Jesus refused the temptation of using His God card to make life easier for Himself.

Jesus was not a superhuman. But He was fully human. *He was a man as God intended man to be.* As we will see in a future lesson, Jesus was the second Adam who did what the first Adam failed to do. For this reason Jesus is our model (pattern) for life and ministry. He shows us what humanity should be like. He shows us what our priorities should be. He shows us how to live in this world without being a part of it. Truly, Jesus was human as God intended us to be.[6]

Dick Staub records how he came to this realization in his book *About You*:

> I came to see Jesus as the great humanizer. I realized that He did not come to start a new religion; He came to rehumanize dehumanized humans, to restore the luster of God's image so we can again glow with God's holistic presence spiritually, intellectually, creatively, morally, and relationally. Jesus came to earth to restore fallen humans to *fully human* beings regardless of their ethnicity, nationality, gender, and economic, educational, or social status.[7]

The model of Jesus' life shows us what being fully human looks like, breaking us out of our sinful ways. We now need to closely examine the model of Jesus' life. Looking closely at the character and priorities of Jesus will provide the key to knowing how to walk as He walked.

FOR DEEPER REFLECTION

Read Philippians 2:5–16 aloud. How does this passage begin and end? Who does it say we are to model? Have the same mindset of Christ Jesus.

What does this passage say about Christ's humanity? What does it say about His deity? He became human so that we would be saved from our sins. So that every knee would bow + acknowledge him as God.

What are the implications of the quote above from Dick Staub? Jesus is our example of how to live fully human lives.

Was Jesus Fully God? DAY 1

The majority of this study will focus on the humanity of Jesus. Before we move on, though, we must begin by clearly establishing the deity of Jesus. The Scripture passages below testify to Christ's deity. Look up each of them and write down what they say about His deity.

John 1:1–3

He was in the beginning and was with God. Through him all things were made.

John 5:16–18

He was persecuted. He worked by the power of his father. Equality with God.

John 5:31–37

He didn't testify about himself. John did it for him. The works he did on earth show his deity.

John 10:30, 38

Jesus + God are 1.

Colossians 1:15–18

He is the image of God. He was part of creation. He holds all things together. He is the head of the church.

Hebrews 1:1–3

Radiance of God's glory.
Representation of God.

Jesus clearly claimed that He was God. People worshiped Jesus as God and He never refused their worship. The reason the Jewish officials crucified Jesus was because His bold claims to be God sounded to them like blasphemy. Never doubt it: Jesus was fully God. Tomorrow we will discover that Jesus was not only fully God, but He was also fully man.

FOR DEEPER REFLECTION

What are some of the implications of Jesus being fully God?

What can happen in our Christian life if we fail to understand that Jesus was fully God?

Was Jesus Fully Human? DAY 2

Scripture is clear—Jesus was fully God. The Scriptures are equally clear that Jesus was also fully human, which means that He was man as God intended man to be. As we will see later, Jesus, as the second Adam, was more like Adam before Adam's fall than He is like us in our fallen state. Look up the following passages and write down what they teach us about Jesus' humanity:

Isaiah 53:1–3

Felt pain. He was despised and rejected.

> **Jesus was God and man in one person, that God and man might be happy together again.**
>
> **—George Whitefield**

Matthew 4:2

He was hungry.

Luke 2:6–7, 11

He was born a natural birth.

Luke 2:52

Jesus grew in wisdom and stature.

John 4:4–7

He was tired and thirsty.

John 11:35

Jesus wept. (cried)

John 19:30, 33

He died,

Philippians 2:7

made himself nothing
took the nature of a servant.
made in human likeness

Hebrews 2:14 and 17

Fully human

> It pleases the Father that all fullness should be in Christ; therefore there is nothing but emptiness anywhere else.
>
> —William Gadsby

Jesus was not *just* human. He was so completely human that those who were closest to Him had the hardest time believing He was the Messiah (Matthew 13:54–56). Indeed He may have been far more average in appearance than many of us would have expected. After all, Isaiah 53:2 says that there "was nothing in his appearance that we should desire him." Jesus hungered and wept and thirsted and even looked like us, so that we might recognize our need to be like Him.

FOR DEEPER REFLECTION

Which of the above passages about Jesus' humanity is most difficult for you to understand? Explain why.

Read Matthew 13:53–56 aloud. Why do you think those closest to Jesus had the hardest time believing He was the Messiah? What does this tell us about His humanity?

DAY 3 Jesus and Miracles

Jesus walked on water, calmed storms with a word, and turned a few loaves and fish into a feast for five thousand. He healed the lame and raised the dead. Don't the miraculous feats Jesus performed prove that He used the God card? How else could He have done such remarkable things? This is a very important question and one that deserves close biblical scrutiny.

Many assume that the miracles proved Jesus was God because only God can do miracles. Today we are going to challenge that assumption.

According to Jesus, where did His power to perform miracles come from? Look closely at John 10:31–32 and 38:

_____

_____

_____

Look also at Acts 2:22 and 10:38. Who performed these miracles?

_____

_____

_____

Check out Luke 5:17. How did Jesus perform the miracles?

_____

_____

_____

It is recorded that Jesus performed over thirty miracles. To the surprise of many, the miracles do not prove His deity as much as they prove that He was the Messiah. What does the Scripture say concerning the coming Messiah? What would the signs of the Messiah be?

Luke 4:18−21

_____

_____

_____

When John the Baptist had been in prison for almost a year, he sent his disciples to Jesus to ask Him if He was the coming Messiah or if they should be looking for someone else. Read Luke 7:20−22. What proof did Jesus give to John that He was the coming Messiah?

_____

_____

_____

Interestingly, the disciples also performed many of the same miracles as Jesus. However, these miracles did not prove that the disciples were divine. On the contrary, they proved that Jesus was alive and well and working through them. Jesus always acknowledged that His Father worked miracles through Him (as a dependent human). In the same way, the disciples always acknowledged that it was Jesus who performed their miracles through them by the Holy Spirit. What does Acts 3:11−16 tell us about the source of miracles?

_____

_____

_____

In our humanity, we are simply vessels for God's power. This is what Jesus modeled for us and taught His disciples. Jesus always acknowledged His Father as the source of His power. Likewise, the disciples acknowledged Jesus as the source of their power. What does this tell us about how a fully human person is to live?

_____

_____

_____

FOR DEEPER REFLECTION

When Jesus performed a miracle, whom did He acknowledge as the source of His power? What does this tell us about true humanity?

As you reflect on the above study, how does this change your view of Jesus and/or true humanity?

Jesus and Knowledge DAY 4

On more than one occasion in the Gospels, Jesus seems to demonstrate supernatural knowledge. For example, He knows what people are thinking before they speak (Mark 2:8; Luke 5:22, 6:8). Isn't this evidence that Jesus used His God card to know things in advance? Not necessarily. Today, we want to look at another possible option.

John 13 records some things that Jesus knew in advance. Read through this chapter and identify three things from verses 1–11.

_____

_____

_____

First Jesus says He "knew that the time had come" to leave the world. Second, verse 3 says, "Jesus knew that the Father had put all things under his power." Finally, Jesus knew who was going to betray Him. Can you think of any way Jesus could have known these things without using His God card?

_____

_____

_____

Maybe the Father revealed these truths to Jesus in advance, through the Spirit of God or the Word of God. What do the following verses tell us about God's desire to reveal things to His children?

Proverbs 3:32

_____

_____

_____

> Not only do we not know God except through Jesus Christ; we do not even know ourselves except through Jesus Christ.
>
> —**Blaise Pascal**

Amos 3:7

_____

_____

_____

Could it be that the God of the universe revealed these things to Jesus because He was "full of the Holy Spirit," "led by the Spirit," and "in the power of the Spirit" (Luke 4:1, 14)? Just because Jesus knew something in advance doesn't mean He used the God card to acquire that knowledge.

Remember, He was fully human and became like us in every way. Just as the Spirit of God revealed things to Jesus, so the Spirit of God can reveal things to us if we are led by the Spirit and walk in the Spirit. Dependence on the Spirit of God and the Word of God empowered Jesus to know things in advance.

What does Luke 24:27 and John 19:28 tell us about where Jesus' knowledge came from?

_____

_____

_____

On several different occasions Jesus was recorded as knowing something in advance.

On four occasions He knew people's thoughts (Matthew 12:24–25, Mark 2:6–8, Luke 6:7–8, Luke 11:16–17). Do these occurrences mean that He used His divinity to know their thoughts? Couldn't His Father have revealed their thoughts to Him? Perhaps He sensed by the countenance of their faces or their body language what they were thinking. Doesn't Proverbs say that the Lord takes the upright into His confidence (Proverbs 3:32)? Amos 3:7 tells us that the "Sovereign Lord does nothing without revealing his plan to his servants . . ." Surely the Spirit of God can give a discerning edge to know people's hearts.

On three occasions it says that Jesus "knew what was in men" (John 2:23–24) or "knew their hypocrisy" (Mark 12:15). Couldn't a mature believer who understands the scriptural teaching about man make these statements?

Just because Jesus knew something in advance, we shouldn't automatically conclude He used His God card to do so.

FOR DEEPER REFLECTION

What do Proverbs 3:32 and Amos 3:7 tell us about God's desire to relate to us personally? What does this tell us about God's character?

Describe a time when the Lord revealed His plan to you in advance. How have you learned to discern whether that plan is from the Spirit? (Consider Acts 13:2–3 and Acts 15:27.)

DAY 5 Jesus, the Second Adam

Scripture tells us that God created Adam from the dust of the earth, formed him in the image of God, and breathed into his nostrils the breath of life. Then God gave him dominion over His creation. For the first time God declared something was "not good." What was this and how did God remedy it (Genesis 2:18–22)? *Man should not be alone.*

He created helpers
suitable for him. Animals
were not suitably enoughs
Eve was created.

Man was alone and without a partner suitable for him, so God made Eve as a helper for him. Adam and Eve were fully human. They walked with God without sin in their life. They had a perfect job, working and caring for the garden of Eden. They had a perfect marriage with a companion created especially for each other. They had a perfect devotional life, as they walked with God Himself in the garden (Genesis 1–2). They were blessed by God and fruitful in every area of their life.

The life Adam and Eve experienced in the Garden, was how God intended man to live. This lasted until Eve sinned and influenced Adam to do the same. Consequently, they ceased to be fully human, that is, as God had made humans to be. They became sinful humans with a sinful nature. Sin permeated Adam and Eve's life and they were cut off from God. Death became a part of their surroundings. Shame became part of their daily experience. God's creation began to groan under the consequences of sin. Adam and Eve's eyes were opened to the reality of life apart from God (Genesis 3). What they once saw clearly they now saw as "a poor reflection as in a mirror" (1 Corinthians 13:12).

For a period of time, Adam and Eve experienced a fully human lifestyle as God intended man to live. What aspect of that perfectly human lifestyle, unmarred by sin, do you most long for?

perfect devotional life

Adam, who once was fully human, became a depraved human, and he passed on to his descendants an inheritance of death and depravity (Romans 5:12). As a result, we now see life through a cloudy lens, influenced by a nature that is distant from God and self-centered at its core. We enjoy darkness and shy from the light and only see beauty and perfection in muted tones. We are no longer fully human—we are sinful humans.

Enter Jesus, God's only Son. He is the second Adam, who brings the life-giving Spirit (1 Corinthians 15:45). Consider this paradox: Adam was placed in paradise and still failed to remain faithful. Jesus, on the other hand, lived in a sin-soaked world, yet He lived an abundant and fully human lifestyle and always chose obedience—including obedience to death on the cross (Philippians 2:8b), providing atonement for the sins of mankind. Through His perfect obedience, He became the Lamb of God who took away the sins of the world. Being the God-Man, He did what Adam could not do: He reversed the consequences of a sin-filled life. Jesus was the last Adam—fully human—so that we, too, one day would become fully human again. He became what He was not, so that we could become what we are not: fully human beings reflecting the full glory of God's creative genius.

In that humanity, He showed us how a fully human person lives life. He painted a clear picture of how to live life in a way that always pleases the Father (see John 5:30). And He calls us to walk as He walked.

So often we make the mistake of defining Jesus' humanity by describing Him through the lens of our sinful human nature. In reality the opposite should be true. Jesus defines what true humanity should look like. Jesus was more like Adam before he sinned, than He was like us in our sin. *We need to see in Jesus the model of how true humanity is to be lived out.* While we will never be sinless like Jesus was . . . as we mature we should sin less, thus becoming more fully human. Jesus is our model for life and ministry.

Return to these Scriptures and reflect upon their truths. Write down their new meaning to you as you reflect upon what Christ did for you.

1 Corinthians 15:20–22

He died and was risen.

1 Corinthians 15:45–57

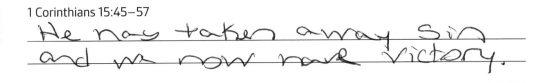

He has taken away sin and we now have victory.

FOR DEEPER REFLECTION

Reread Hebrews 2:14–3:1 aloud. What does this passage say to you about Christ's humanity?

What aspects of Christ's humanity are most difficult for you to grasp?

What questions do you still have about Christ's humanity?

WEEKS 1 AND 2 SUMMARY

1. Jesus is our model for life and ministry, and we are commanded to "walk as He walked."

2. In His humanity, Jesus was man as God intended mankind to be, showing us how to walk.

WEEKS **3-8** : AN OVERVIEW

FOUNDATIONAL PRIORITIES

IN JESUS' LIFE AND MINISTRY

For a few years, the John Hancock Center stood in downtown Chicago as the world's tallest building.

At the peak of the construction, over 2,000 people worked on the project, which required some 5,000,000 man-hours to complete. Enough steel was used in the frame alone to make over 33,000 cars. Each of the four corner columns weighs nearly 100 tons each. Every day the building's 1,250 miles of wiring uses enough electricity to power a city of 30,000 people.

But the most significant part of the John Hancock Center is not its unique design, nor the innovative construction methods that were developed to bring the project to completion, nor the massive amount of resources it requires today. The most significant aspect of the building is its immense foundation. Because the building stands in the soft ground near Lake Michigan, the building's engineers had to sink massive caissons into 10-foot holes drilled 190 feet into the bedrock. Without a solid foundation, all the work of building this impressive structure would have been in vain. The designers took no chances. They understood that a structure is only as good as its foundation.

As it is with construction, so it is with our lives and ministry. Our success depends upon the integrity of our foundation. So, for the next few weeks, we'll be looking at six foundational priorities upon which Jesus built His life and ministry. They are: (1) dependence upon the Holy Spirit, (2) a life of fervent prayer, (3) obedience to His Father's kingdom agenda, (4) the centrality of the Word, (5) exalting His Father always, and (6) intentional relationships with His disciples and the crowds. It may help you to remember these priorities if you think of them as the acronym **Holy Spirit POWER**:

Holy Spirit DEPENDENCE
PRAYERFUL GUIDANCE
OBEDIENT LIVING
WORD-CENTERED
EXALTING THE FATHER
RELATIONAL INTENTIONALITY

These foundational priorities will help us understand *how* Jesus lived and walked. In Jesus we will see what it means to be fully human . . . to experience life to its full (John 10:10). These foundational priorities will help us practically understand what it means to "walk as Jesus walked."

JESUS AND THE HOLY SPIRIT

See WalkingAsJesus.com for video resources specific to this week's study.

GETTING STARTED

I had studied the life of Christ for years before I noticed the central role the Holy Spirit played in Jesus' life. I recognized the intimate relationship between Jesus and the Father. However, a closer look at the Scriptures helped me realize that every aspect of Christ's ministry was saturated with the presence and power of the Holy Spirit.

Christ's very birth was a work of the Holy Spirit. Luke tells us that Jesus was conceived by the Holy Spirit. The angel told Mary that she would become pregnant when the "Holy Spirit will come upon you, and the power of the Most High will overshadow you. So the holy one to be born will be called the Son of God" (Luke 1:35).

When Jesus was approximately thirty years old, He obviously became aware that the fullness of time had arrived when He should be baptized by His cousin John in the Jordan River, about eighty miles away. Could this realization have been the leading of the Holy Spirit? At His baptism, John recognized Jesus as the sent one when the Holy Spirit came "down and remain[ed] on Him" (John 1:33). Not only was Jesus baptized with water; He was also baptized "with the Holy Spirit."

Immediately thereafter, Jesus was "led by the Spirit" to spend forty days in the wilderness. Toward the end of this period He was tempted by Satan. Luke emphatically records that Jesus entered the desert full of the Holy Spirit and He came out of the desert and "returned to Galilee in the power of the Spirit" (Luke 4:14).

Later the Scriptures tell us that Jesus was anointed by the Spirit (Luke 4:18, Acts 10:38), sent by the Spirit, did miracles by the Spirit (Matthew 12:28), and preached in the power of the Spirit. He also rejoiced in the Spirit (Luke 10:21) and gave instruction "through the Holy Spirit" (Acts 1:2). John's gospel records that Jesus received the "seal of approval" (6:27) from His Father, an obvious reference to the Holy Spirit's presence (also see Ephesians 1:13).

The Scriptures make clear that after Jesus gave His life on the cross, He was raised by the Spirit (Romans 8:11).

The Holy Spirit's guidance and power marked every aspect of Christ's life. In His humanity, Jesus understood that being fully human meant that by Himself, He could "do nothing" (John 5:19 and 30). After modeling a life of dependence on the Holy Spirit, Jesus told us that in the same way, "apart from me you can do nothing" (John 15:5). Learning dependence on the Holy Spirit, then, is a crucial aspect of learning to walk as Jesus walked.

Read Luke 4:1–21 and list the ways in which you see the Holy Spirit's role in Jesus' life.

He ate nothing for 40 days. Resisted / Temptation. Overcome temptations. He announced the prophecy from Isaiah is fulfilled.

FOR DEEPER REFLECTION

Read aloud each of the other verses above that describe Jesus and the Holy Spirit. Which is most amazing to you?

If Jesus in His humanity acknowledged His need for the Holy Spirit, what does this tell us about our need for the Holy Spirit?

The Holy Spirit and Growth DAY 1

Jesus' earthly life began with a miraculous demonstration of the power of the Holy Spirit. Read the familiar story of the annunciation of Jesus' birth in Luke 1:26–35. Imagine afresh the impact this appearance must have had on the young Mary. What do you think Mary thought and felt as she pondered the angel's announcement?

_____

_____

_____

What role did the Holy Spirit play in bringing life into Mary's womb? Isn't it also true that we are unable to have spiritual life within us apart from the Holy Spirit? Write out John 3:5–9. How is the birth of Jesus similar to our "second" birth?

_____

_____

_____

Later in Luke's gospel, we read that the child Jesus "grew and became strong; he was filled with wisdom, and the grace of God was upon Him" (Luke 2:40; also see verse 52). As Gerald Hawthorne writes,

> The participle *pleroumenon* is in the passive voice meaning that Jesus was being filled by someone! That is to say, someone other than Jesus himself was doing the filling. But who? Luke does not say in just so many words who this agent was. One may infer, however, both from what Luke had to say earlier about the agent at Jesus' birth (1:35), and from what he will say later on about the driving force in Jesus' ministry (4:1), that this unnamed agent was none other than the Holy Spirit.[1]

How do you think the Spirit of God continually filled Jesus with wisdom? What things might Jesus have done that allowed the Holy Spirit to work in Him during His childhood? (Read Luke 2:51–52 and 4:16, and use your sanctified imagination to think this through.)

_____

_____

_____

The process of spiritual growth

Is it possible to grow spiritually apart from the work of the Holy Spirit? Many of us behave as if we believe we can grow spiritually if we just work hard, study hard, or try hard. We think that by reading words on a page we can get to know God, or that by attending church faithfully for years, we can grow to be like Him. Isaiah 55:8–9 tells a different story. Open your Bible and write down what Isaiah is saying in this passage.

_____

_____

_____

Look also at Zechariah 4:6. What are the implications of this statement for you and me?

_____

_____

_____

The Scriptures tell us that in and of ourselves we cannot please God and are completely unable to comprehend the ways of God. How does Colossians 2:13 describe our spiritual condition?

_____

_____

_____

To what extent is a dead person able to grow spiritually? Explain your answer.

_____

_____

_____

How does Romans 8:9–14 explain our solution to this problem?

_____

_____

_____

Hindering the work of the Spirit

If Jesus, in His humanity, needed the Spirit of God to grow, what does this tell us about our desperate need for the Holy Spirit in our lives?

_____

_____

_____

How can we experience the work of the Holy Spirit in our lives (see Ephesians 5:18)? Explain your understanding of how to do this.

_____

_____

_____

Paul speaks of "grieving" (Ephesians 4:30) or "quenching" (1 Thessalonians 5:18 NASB) the Spirit of God. What word pictures come to your mind when you think of grieving or quenching the Spirit?

_____

_____

_____

FOR DEEPER REFLECTION

Write out your understanding of how to "keep in step" with the Holy Spirit. (See Galatians 5:25.)

What are some practical ways we deny our need for the Holy Spirit? (See Zechariah 4:6.)

What are some ways in which we hinder the Holy Spirit? (See Ephesians 4:29–32.)

DAY 2 The Holy Spirit and Guidance

Jesus' ministry—His very life—was inaugurated by the Holy Spirit. Moreover, the Scriptures clearly tell us that Jesus was "led by the Spirit" throughout His life (Luke 4:1). Stop for a moment to think about what this indicates about the humanity of Christ. Reflect on Luke 4 and write down how you understand the role of the Spirit in Jesus' life.

Guides his every move.

In Luke 4:1, where did the Spirit lead Jesus and what did Jesus face there? What are the implications of this in our relationship with the Holy Spirit?

Wilderness to face the devil. We should rely on the Spirit when we are in a wilderness.

Because we know that Jesus in His humanity never sinned, we know that Jesus was always "led by the Spirit," always walking "in step with the Spirit." Below are a few passages that indicate that Jesus listened to the Spirit of God. How do these verses show us that Jesus was obviously listening to the Holy Spirit?

John 4:4 (No good Jew would go through Samaria because of the Samaritans . . . what does this tell us about Jesus and His sensitivity to the Spirit? What happened in Samaria?)

The spirit led him through Samaria because otherwise he wouldn't have gone.

John 5:6 (See also Acts 10:38.)

Normally you don't heal on the Sabbath.

John 6:5–6

The H.S. already talked to him.

John 6:63–65

He knew how to react even though Judas betrayed him.

John 7:14–16

The H.S. taught him the Scriptures.

John 11:3–6

The H.S. prompted Jesus to wait 2 days. Timing.

Matthew 16:21

With him, even in death.

Our listening to the Holy Spirit

The common phrase used for each of the seven churches in the book of Revelation is found in Revelation 2:7, 11, 17, 29 and 3:6, 13, 22. What is that command given to each of the seven churches? Write it below:

Whoever has ears, let them hear what the Spirit says to the churches.

What would you say is required of us to properly hear what the Spirit is saying?

Spending time with the Spirit. Learning his voice.

What insight does Hebrews 5:14 give us about learning to listen to what the Spirit is saying? How does it suggest that we become mature?

We need to learn & be trained.

FOR DEEPER REFLECTION

According to the verses above, how were Jesus' life and ministry affected when He took time to listen to the Holy Spirit?

Acts 1:1–2 can be understood in a couple of different ways. One way of looking at Acts 1:1–2 suggests that there was a period of time when the disciples needed to learn to get their instructions from the Holy Spirit rather than directly from the physical Jesus. What unique lessons may they have needed to learn in order to begin to listen to the Spirit's voice?

The Holy Spirit and Power DAY 3

In our last session we saw that the Holy Spirit led Jesus into the desert to confront the devil. In Luke 4:14, we are told that Jesus "returned to Galilee in the power of the Spirit, and news about him spread through the whole countryside." The Greek word for power is *dunamis*, from which we get our English word "dynamite." What picture does this paint for you of Jesus' return to Galilee?

_____

_____

_____

Why do you think a new season of Holy Spirit power often follows a desert experience in our lives? What happens in the desert that enables the Spirit to work? (See Deuteronomy 8:1–5.)

_____

_____

_____

> **There is no worse screen to block out the Spirit than confidence in our own intelligence.**
>
> **—John Calvin**

After His return to Galilee, Jesus traveled to Nazareth, where He grew up (Luke 4:16). He went to the synagogue to worship, as usual. But this time He opened the scroll and read from Isaiah. Read Luke 4:18 and Isaiah 61:1–2. What did Isaiah prophesy regarding how the power of the Holy Spirit would manifest itself in the Messiah?

_____

_____

_____

As we discussed in Week 2, the miracles do not prove the deity of Jesus. Instead they prove His messiahship, as Isaiah 61:1–2 indicates. When John the Baptist had spent awhile in prison, he began to question who Jesus really was. He sent his disciples to ask Jesus if He was the Messiah, or if they should be looking for someone else. In His response, Jesus referenced most of Isaiah 61:1–2 again. But He left out one aspect of it. See if you can find what He left out. Compare Luke 7:22–23 with Luke 4:18–19.

_____

_____

_____

Ephesians 3:16–19 speaks twice of the power of the Spirit of God. How is the power of the Holy Spirit realized in these verses? What is the result of the Holy Spirit's power in our lives?

_____

_____

_____

On the other hand, what can we assume will happen if we grieve or quench the Spirit's power in our lives?

_____

_____

_____

Jesus was totally yielded to the Father's will, a sinless and pure vessel dedicated to the Father's work; "streams of living water" (John 7:38) flowed through Him. In the same way, if we walk in the power of the Holy Spirit, with no known sin in our life, God can also work through us. Do you believe God still wants to do the "supernatural" through His children? (See John 16:24.)

_____

_____

_____

Rate on a scale of 1–10 your confidence that God wants to work supernaturally through you:

little confidence		some confidence		growing confidence			great confidence	
1	2	3	4	5	6	7	8	9	10

During His last discourse with His disciples in the upper room, Jesus told His disciples six times to "ask." What did He tell them to ask for and how were they to ask? (See John 14:14, 15:7 and 16, and 16:23, 24, and 26.)

_____

_____

_____

FOR DEEPER REFLECTION

Jesus tells us to "ask" for some amazing things. What might happen if we took Jesus at His word? (See an example of this in John 4:50.)

In what ways do you underestimate what Jesus wants to accomplish through you? What keeps you from taking Jesus at His word and asking for even greater things (John 16:24)?

DAY 4 The Holy Spirit and Joy

When you imagine the human Jesus, what picture first surfaces in your mind? Do you visualize Him as a sorrowful person, deeply burdened by the profound needs of the people around Him? Or do you visualize Him smiling and joyful in spirit? Do you ever picture Him joking playfully with His disciples, or do you suspect He was always sober and serious? Your view of Jesus often determines the type of person you strive to become.

> As the sun can be seen only by its own light, so Christ can be known only by His own Spirit.
>
> —Robert Leighton

The Scriptures testify that Jesus was "full of joy" (Luke 10:21). What does this mean? What does it look like?

Three times Scripture records that Jesus wept. Each occasion was within the last few weeks of His earthly ministry. We see Him weeping over Lazarus in John 11:35. We see Him weeping over Jerusalem during Passion Week, as He enters the city for the final time as the triumphant Messiah. And then finally, we see Him in the garden of Gethsemane where with "loud cries and tears to the one who could save him from death " (Hebrews 5:7), He pleaded, "Father, if you are willing, take this cup from me; yet not my will, but yours be done" (Luke 22:42). The final few weeks of Jesus' life were an emotional time for Him and His disciples.

As these passages indicate, Jesus was indeed "a man of sorrows, and familiar with suffering" (Isaiah 53:3). Jesus knew and fully understood human grief. Yet too often we allow this quality of Jesus to paint our primary image of Him. Jesus was also called a friend of sinners (Matthew 11:19). What made Him attractive to sinners? Was He always sorrowful? Or was there something different about Jesus that made Him attractive to the "tax collectors and 'sinners' "?

Look at Hebrews 1:9. Hebrews quotes the psalmist, who writes that the Messiah will be exalted above His companions. What is the key ingredient that sets Him above others?

_____

_____

_____

What does this tell us about the person of Jesus when He walked on this earth? One Bible translation says He was anointed "by pouring out the oil of joy on you more than on anyone else" (NLT). If Jesus was exalted above His companions because of His joy and gladness, wouldn't this be evident in His demeanor (Proverbs 15:13a)? Could it be that while Jesus was a man acquainted with sorrow, He was also inviting and joyful? As you meditate on this verse, how does it shape your view of Jesus?

_____

_____

_____

Do you know where Jesus performed His first recorded miracle? (Hint: John 2:1–11) Notice how extravagant it was for Him to turn 180 gallons of water into "the best" wine at the wedding. What does this tell us about Jesus' attitude about life?

_____

_____

_____

In Luke 15 Jesus asks rhetorically whether salt can ever be made salty again. If there is an answer, it is found in Luke 15:1–3. Where do you find Jesus? Who is sitting nearest to Him? What was it about Jesus' character and personality that made Him so winsome to the lost?

_____

_____

_____

We know that joy is a fruit of the Holy Spirit. We also know that Jesus had the Holy Spirit without limit (John 3:34). So it should not surprise us that Luke records in 10:21 that Jesus was "full of joy." Yet the context of this verse is powerful. At this point Jesus was three and a half years into His public ministry, right near the end of it. For over three years Jesus had poured His life into His disciples. His personal calling was to die for the sins of the world, but His ministry focus for His disciples was to equip them to walk as He walked, sharing their faith with others in the power of the Spirit. In Luke 9, Jesus sends out the twelve apostles two by two. In Luke 10 He sends out seventy-two next generation leaders two by two. They go out preaching that people everywhere should repent, for the kingdom of God is near. They return full of joy. Jesus, too, was "full of joy" by the Holy Spirit. Why?

_____

_____

_____

Could it be that Jesus' mission was not to reach the world, as much as it was to make disciples who could reach the world? Jesus knew that for us to be here today as His followers would require that He equip His disciples to make disciples who could make disciples. Jesus' mission was to create a movement of multiplying disciples. His joy was rooted in multiplication and reproduction. As you study the life of Christ you will find that Jesus spent more time with His disciples than He did with the masses, teaching and investing in them.

Think about your own life. Are you "walking as Jesus walked" by investing in others? Write below the names of the people you are investing in regularly.

_____

_____

_____

FOR DEEPER REFLECTION

How could Jesus be known both as a "man of sorrows" and "full of joy"?

When you think of Jesus, what is your primary view of Him—a man of sorrows or full of joy?

Why? What might change if you viewed Jesus differently?

Friendship with the Holy Spirit DAY 5

Scripture has different ways of commanding us to walk as Jesus walked. One powerful way is through the "as" or "just as" verses in the Bible. For example: "Whoever wants to be first must be your slave—*just as* the Son of man did not come to be served, but to serve" (Matthew 20:27–28). "*Just as* the living Father sent me and I live because of the Father, so the one who feeds on me will live because of me" (John 6:57). "*As* the living Father sent me, so I am sending you" (John 20:21). These are remarkable challenges to live life *just as* Jesus did.

Jesus gives His disciples another—perhaps the most difficult—"just as" command in John 13. He tells them, "Love one another. *As* I have loved you, so you must love one another" (John 13:34). But along with this command Jesus also suggests how it will be possible for the disciples to behave just like Jesus. He is going away, He explains; but they should not be troubled, because He is leaving for their good. Jesus intends to give "another Counselor to be with you forever, the Spirit of truth" (John 14:16–17).

The word translated "counselor" (*parakaleo*, "the one who comes alongside") can also be translated as "comforter" or "helper." But this might not be the most important word in the verse. What does it mean that Jesus would send *another* counselor? The original counselor was the Wonderful Counselor of Isaiah 9:6, Jesus Himself.

The word translated "another" in John 14:15 is the Greek word *allos*, which means another of the exact same kind. The Greek word *heteros* means "another of a different kind." For example, apples and oranges are both fruits, but they are *heteros* fruits—fruits of different kinds. Apples and apples, by contrast, are *allos* fruits or "fruits of exactly the same kind." We might expect John to use the word *heteros* to describe the helper Jesus would send. Surely this new helper could not be exactly like Jesus. But John chose the word *allos* on purpose, to emphasize that the Holy Spirit would be for the Twelve, and for us, a guide exactly like the man Jesus.

I have often wondered what it would be like to be one of the original twelve disciples who literally walked with Jesus. *If only I could have been one of the Twelve*, I have often thought, *it would have been far easier to follow Jesus faithfully*. The truth of John 14:16 is that if we have fellowship

WALKING AS JESUS WALKED

with the Holy Spirit, we have access to a counselor *just like Jesus*. Walking with the Spirit is just like walking with the physical Jesus.

But there's more.

John traces the progression of the disciples' relationship with Jesus throughout his book. The disciples began as seekers (John 1:39), became followers (John 1:43), and then fellow servants (John 13:16). Finally Jesus calls them friends (John 15:15). Friends with Jesus! That's no small calling!

Now Jesus tells His disciples that they will have the same relationship with the Holy Spirit. Just as Jesus had grown to call His disciples friends, so too would the Holy Spirit. Just as Jesus was to the Twelve, the Holy Spirit is to us today. What amazing news! Is the Holy Spirit your best friend?

What does friendship look like? What would friendship with the Holy Spirit involve?

_____

_____

_____

How would your view of the Holy Spirit change if you believed that He desired to be your friend, just as Jesus was to the Twelve?

_____

_____

_____

Acts 15:28 sheds light on this subject. Faced with a problem, the leadership of the early church goes behind closed doors to discuss the issue and seek solutions. How do they explain their relationship with the Holy Spirit? What does this tell us about our relationship with the Spirit?

_____

_____

_____

The Holy Spirit is mentioned over fifty times in the book of Acts. The Holy Spirit was to the New Testament church what Jesus had been to the Twelve. The Holy Spirit was their friend, guiding

> **Faith in Christ makes one a regenerated believer; obedience to the Holy Spirit makes him a spiritual believer.**
>
> —Watchman Nee

them as Jesus guided the Twelve, teaching them as Jesus taught the Twelve, encouraging them as Jesus encouraged the Twelve. It was important that Jesus ascend to heaven so that we each could know the presence of the Holy Spirit in our lives. Is the Holy Spirit your friend? He longs to be.

FOR DEEPER REFLECTION

What would change if we viewed the Holy Spirit as the disciples viewed Jesus?

How have you seen the Holy Spirit guide you? In what area do you need some guidance right now?

Share an example of when you experienced the power or leading of the Holy Spirit.

Read through the book of Acts and try to identify the fifty-plus times where the Holy Spirit is mentioned (or use an online study tool). Learn from these verses how the Holy Spirit interfaced with the New Testament believers.

WEEKS 1–3 SUMMARY

1. Jesus is our model for life and ministry, and we are commanded to "walk as He walked."

2. In His humanity, Jesus was man as God intended mankind to be, showing us how to walk.

3. The first foundational priority we see in Jesus' humanity was total dependence on the Holy Spirit in everything He did.

PRAYING AS JESUS PRAYED

See WalkingAsJesus.com for video resources specific to this week's study.

GETTING STARTED

In the previous unit we established the central importance of the Holy Spirit for walking as Jesus walked. The Holy Spirit is a counselor and guide for us *just like* the physical Jesus was for the Twelve. One way we demonstrate our dependence on the Spirit is by developing personal habits and practices that give the Spirit opportunity to work in our lives.

When I first began to study the life of Christ, I was quickly amazed at the prayer life of Jesus. The Scriptures record thirty-three different instances in which Jesus takes time to pray.[1] Christ's ministry began with prayer (Luke 3:21) and ended with prayer (Mark 15:38–39). Jesus prayed before every major turning point in His life. Before every major crisis, He slipped away to pray. The busier Jesus became the more He prayed.

Prayer was central to who Jesus was, central to His being fully human. It was a way for Jesus to renew His energy and determine His next step. Prayer was a priority that at times demanded that He withdraw from the crowds to communicate with the Father.

Jesus' disciples knew that His prayer life was what made Him different from all the other leaders. Never did they ask, "Lord, teach us to do miracles" or, "Teach us to preach like You do." But they did ask Jesus to teach them to pray.

WALKING AS JESUS WALKED

In this unit, we will study the prayer life of Jesus. The goal is not to make us feel guilty, but to learn from the Master. Someone has said that if you want to make people feel guilty, just talk about prayer or evangelism. It doesn't matter how much we are praying or how much we are evangelizing, we usually feel we ought to be doing more. Our goal is to look closely at Jesus' prayer life so we can glean lessons to adapt in our own busy lifestyles.

> You can do more than pray after you have prayed; but you can never do more than pray until you have prayed.
>
> —A. J. Gordon

Whole books and seminars have been devoted to this topic, so there is much we could say. This section focuses specifically on Jesus' prayer life—how He prayed in His humanity—and what that means for us as we try to walk as He walked. We will not cover a lot of new material; but I hope you will see how Jesus, the second Adam, modeled a lifestyle of prayer and gain a fresh passion for praying as Jesus prayed.

When you think of Jesus and prayer, which stories or passages immediately come to your mind? Record as many as you can below.

_____
_____
_____
_____
_____
_____

Prayer and Direction DAY 1

The very first reference to prayer in Jesus' life appears at the beginning of His ministry. What does the Bible say happened "as he was praying" in Luke 3:21–23?

_____

_____

_____

Mark also records Jesus' baptism in his gospel. As Jesus was coming up out of the Jordan River, Mark 1:10 tells us, He saw heaven "being torn open." The Greek word translated "torn" (*schizo*) appears again in Mark 15:38. It is similar to the Hebrew word *qara'* used in Isaiah 64:1–3. What's happening in these other passages of Scripture? What does this suggest about what God the Father is doing at Jesus' baptism?

_____

_____

_____

Then the Father speaks from heaven, "You are my Son, whom I love; with you I am well pleased" (Luke 3:22). These words are directed to Jesus! Imagine the impact this must have had on the human Jesus. In their excellent book *Sitting at the Feet of Rabbi Jesus*, Ann Spangler and Lois Tverberg explain that the Father employs a pattern in this proclamation that was very familiar to rabbis at the time. Called "stringing pearls," this way of speaking brought together Scripture passages from different parts of the Old Testament and combines them in a new way in order to reveal great truths. "You are my Son" comes from Psalm 2:7; "whom I love" is from Genesis 22:2; and "with you I am well pleased" is from Isaiah 42:1. As Spangler writes, "In just three brief quotes from the Old Testament Scriptures, God speaks of Jesus as a king, a servant, and his Son, who will become a sacrifice. When God speaks, he packs a lot into his words!"[2]

Jesus had prepared for this moment for thirty years. Could this have been the first time His Father clearly communicated to Him that He was the Messiah? Many people assume that Jesus always knew He was the Messiah. But we shouldn't be too quick to make that assumption. Jesus in His humanity had to learn and grow, just as we must learn and grow, in His understanding of the Father's plan for His life. Of course, Mary likely told Jesus about His miraculous birth and the angels' announcements about His calling and mission. But even she failed to understand the full significance of Jesus' work, even up to the very end of His life. Surely she told Jesus, "You are very special." But I imagine every good Jewish mom said that to her son.

However we understand Luke 3:22, it clearly speaks to a unique calling on Jesus' life. The words are direct ("You are my son"), emotional ("whom I love"), and encouraging ("with you I am well pleased"). If the words themselves were not encouragement enough, the Holy Spirit Himself descended on Jesus as soon as they were spoken. As we discussed in the previous study, the Spirit then led Jesus into the desert (Luke 4:1–13), where He fasted for forty days. While the text does not say explicitly that this was a time of prayer, we know from the Old Testament that fasting and prayer were usually done together.

What kinds of things do you think Jesus discussed in prayer with His Father during these forty days?

_____

_____

_____

Two of the three temptations from Satan began with the taunt "If you are the Son of God." Satan was directly challenging what Jesus' Father had just said to Him at His baptism. Satan hoped Jesus would use His God card to make the challenges ahead easier for Himself. But Jesus refused. Sometimes Satan tries to tempt us to take shortcuts in the wilderness of our lives. He knows that the easy way out is seldom the right way out.

Is there a time in your life when Satan tempted you to take the easy way out? Describe that experience in the space below.

_____

_____

_____

If Jesus spent forty days in prayer and fasting before He launched His ministry, what does this tell us about our ministry? Don't overlook the obvious.

_____

_____

_____

FOR DEEPER REFLECTION

What lessons can we learn from the progression of events surrounding the baptism and temptation of Jesus? Here they are again in outline form:

>   *1. While Jesus is praying . . .*
>
>   *2. the heavens are torn open . . .*
>
>   *3. the Father speaks . . .*
>
>   *4. the Spirit descends and leads . . .*
>
>   *5. Satan tempts . . .*
>
>   *6. angels minister . . .*

Which step(s) do you feel are missing from your life and ministry?

DAY 2 Prayer and Daily Routines

Write out Luke 5:16 below. Take note of every word in this verse.

But Jesus often withdrew to lonely places and prayed.

Early in His ministry, Jesus was led by the Spirit into the wilderness to fast and pray for forty days. Luke 5:16 indicates that prayer was a habitual practice for Jesus, for He "often withdrew to lonely places and prayed." The Greek word translated "lonely" is *eremos*, the same Greek word translated "desert" in Luke 4:1. It is also the same word used in Mark 6:31 when, after a busy day of ministry, Jesus invites His disciples to "Come with me by yourselves to a *quiet place* [*eremos*] and get some rest." Jesus learned early on, under the guidance of the Holy Spirit, the importance of getting away to pray—and doing it *often*! Could it be here that in Mark 6:31 Jesus is teaching His disciples a lesson the Spirit of God had already taught Him about the central importance of spending time alone with the Father?

What does Luke 5:16 indicate about the habits of Jesus?

Often. When he needed refreshment.

If you wanted Jesus, but couldn't find Him, it would be safe to conclude that He might be somewhere in prayer. Read Mark 1:35 and pay attention to the details about how much sleep Jesus had after a busy night (verses 32 and 35). Where did the disciples find Jesus?

a solitary place

> **Don't pray when you feel like it. Have an appointment with the Lord and keep it. A man is powerful on his knees.**
>
> —Corrie ten Boom

On another occasion, Judas tried to find Jesus, too. Read Mark 14:10–11 and Luke 22:39 and 47. How did Judas know where to find Jesus? What does this tell us about Jesus' daily patterns?

It was his usual place.
He had a habit - pattern

Psalm 5:3 speaks beautifully about the value of setting aside time to meet with the Lord daily. What does this verse tell us we should do? What does it suggest God does in response?

Wait expectantly. Listens &
hears our cry.

Do those closest to you know that you "often withdraw to lonely places to pray"? How can your life be adjusted so that your commitment to prayer better imitates Jesus?

Make priority
Spiritual disciplines

FOR DEEPER REFLECTION

According to Psalm 5:7–8,11–12, what are the consequences of a daily dialogue with the Lord?

Joy, protection, blessing

What would it look like in your life if, like Jesus, you were to make it a priority to slip away often to pray? Try to describe it in practical terms.

Focus on God
Inner peace

DAY 3 Prayer and Life Decisions

We learned in the last session that Jesus made a habit of daily prayer. Besides these regular times of communication with the Father, Jesus also dedicated Himself to prayer before every major turning point in His life. This is no coincidence! Prayer changed the trajectory of Jesus' life and ministry on several occasions, and today we are going to explore how.

Prayer—secret, fervent, believing prayer—lies at the root of all personal godliness.

—William Carey

Let's begin by returning to Mark 1:32–39. About eighteen months into Jesus' ministry, after a very busy day, Jesus wakes up early to slip away to pray. Have you ever wondered what Jesus prayed about? What might have He discussed with His Father? Mark 1 gives us some insight into these questions. How did Jesus respond when He found out that "the whole town" was looking for Him?

_____

_____

_____

If you had been in Jesus' sandals that day, how would you have responded? Be honest.

_____

_____

_____

In another interesting passage, after feeding five thousand people, Jesus "made his disciples get into the boat and go on ahead of him to the other side, while he dismissed the crowd. After he had dismissed them, he went up on a mountainside by himself to pray" (Matthew 14:22–23a). In the parallel passage in Mark 6:45–50, the story continues by pointing out that Jesus had been watching from the mountainside as His disciples were "straining at the oars" throughout the late watch of the night. He does something He has never done before. He meets them on the sea, walking on the water. What's more, Jesus allows Peter to participate in the supernatural experience (Matthew 14:28)!

Using your sanctified imagination, what do you think Jesus could have been praying for as He watched His disciples "straining at the oars"?

_____

_____

_____

How did this time of prayer affect Jesus' actions? How did Jesus' actions affect His disciples?

_____

_____

_____

About two and a half years into His ministry Jesus faced a new challenge. The crowds were multiplying, and Jesus knew that He needed to appoint leaders who could preach among the people. In response to this need, Jesus spent an entire night in prayer. Look at Luke 6:12. What can we learn from Jesus' example in this situation?

_____

_____

_____

What do you think Jesus prayed for all night?

_____

_____

_____

FOR DEEPER REFLECTION

What life decisions do you need to pray about? Spend some extended time praying about these life decisions.

DAY 4 Prayer and Life Struggles

Life can be very hard. Jesus knew this full well, for He was not exempt from the struggles of life. As we discussed in a previous lesson, Isaiah called Jesus a "man of sorrows, acquainted with grief." It is easy to think of the difficulties Jesus faced during His ministry—the opposition of religious leaders, the unbelief of neighbors and loved ones, the terrible weight of sin. But Jesus faced difficulties before He launched His ministry. Jesus faced difficulties in the daily patterns of life, just as we do. Psalm 69:7–12 is a messianic passage, which several believe may speak of Jesus' early years, before the beginning of His ministry.

> For I endure scorn for your sake
> and shame covers my face.
> I am a stranger to my brothers,
> an alien to my own mother's sons;
> for zeal for your house consumes me,
> and the insults of those who insult you fall on me.
> When I weep and fast,
> I must endure scorn;
> when I put on sackcloth,
> people make sport of me.
> Those who sit at the gate mock me,
> and I am a song of the drunkards.

What difficulties might Jesus have faced as a young boy growing up in Nazareth? Imagine the pain of hearing schoolmates use God's name in vain. Imagine the ridicule Jesus may have endured from His adolescent classmates as He was becoming a young man. Imagine the distance Jesus may have felt from family members who didn't understand His sensitive spirit.

I imagine Jesus, as a young boy, deeply troubled by people's lack of zeal for His Father's house. As Jesus heard the stories of Daniel, or David, or even Jeremiah, I imagine Jesus imitating these Old Testament prophets by putting on sackcloth to fast and pray—only to be mocked by the townspeople of Nazareth. I imagine the drunkards at the city gate making up songs questioning who Jesus' real dad might be.

Reread this portion of Psalm 69. How does the psalmist describe some of Jesus' life struggles?

_____

_____

_____

How do you imagine Jesus responded in the face of these struggles?

_____

_____

_____

Prayer and personal pain

John the Baptist and Jesus were cousins. We don't know how much time they spent together growing up, but we can assume that their kinship must have increased when John was called to prepare the way for Jesus' ministry. For the first year and a half of John's ministry, he was the Billy Graham of his day. People came to hear him preach from all over Judea. The people's focus on John afforded Jesus the space to spend time with His first disciples (Andrew, Peter, and John—John probably being the second disciple mentioned as he wrote this passage; see John 1:37—and then Philip and Nathanael; see John 1:45 and John 3:22). The ministry of John was crucial for the ministry of Jesus. Imagine the suffering Jesus must have experienced when He heard the news that John had been beheaded in prison. You can read the account in Matthew 14:3–14.

When Jesus heard about John's death, what was His response?

_____

_____

_____

Jesus wanted to get alone, perhaps to process this news of His relative's death with His Father. But the crowds followed Him. In the midst of His personal suffering, how did Jesus respond to the crowds?

_____

_____

_____

It was not until some time later that Jesus was able to get alone on the mountainside to pray (Matthew 14:23). What do you imagine Jesus prayed about that evening?

_____

_____

_____

Prayer and understanding next steps

About nine months before His final journey into Jerusalem for Passover, Jesus took His disciples on a long journey north to Caesarea Philippi (Luke 9:18). Here Jesus "was praying in private and his disciples were with him." He then asked them who people thought He was. Peter confessed that Jesus was the Messiah, and Jesus warned them not to tell anyone.

"From that time on," Matthew 16:21 tells us, "Jesus began to explain to his disciples that he must go to Jerusalem and suffer many things at the hands of the elders, chief priests and teachers of the law, and that he must be killed and on the third day be raised to life." Jesus' teaching took on a new urgency. He began to explain to the disciples the cost of taking up their crosses to follow Him.

Jesus then took Peter, John, and James up onto a mountain to pray (Luke 9:28). There Jesus was transfigured before them, and "Moses and Elijah appeared in glorious splendor, talking with Jesus." What do you think they talked about? Luke tells us they "spoke about his departure" (Luke 9:31). Why do you think the Father sent Moses and Elijah to speak to Jesus about His departure? Perhaps like us, Jesus in His humanity may have needed some encouragement. If Jesus "was tempted in every way, just like we are" (Hebrews 4:15), why might He need the experience of the transfiguration for encouragement and endurance? What insight does Hebrews 12:2 give us? How does this apply to us?

_____

_____

_____

What are you facing right now that you could take some time alone with the Lord to process?

_____

_____

_____

Prayer in the garden . . . alone

How does Jesus describe His experience in the garden of Gethsemane in Matthew 26:37–38?

_____

_____

_____

Why was prayer the solution for Jesus?

_____

_____

_____

What does Hebrews 4:16 tell us that we can find and receive in prayer?

_____

_____

_____

FOR DEEPER REFLECTION

How can we learn obedience through suffering? (Hint: Read Hebrews 5:8.)

How is prayer connected to learning obedience? (See Matthew 26:39 and 42.)

DAY 5 **Prayer and Our Loved Ones**

John 13:1–2 tells us that Jesus "loved his own . . . He . . . showed them the full extent of His love." Who has God placed in your life that you love deeply? They may be your children, parents, friends, neighbors, or coworkers. Identify them below.

_____

_____

_____

In one of the most intimate and lengthy of Jesus' prayers we have recorded, Jesus prays for His disciples. In John 17, Jesus prays at least seven specific things for the disciples He loves. Read John 17 and record seven things Jesus prays for them.

_____

_____

_____

_____

_____

_____

Jesus also identifies at least twelve very practical things that He does for those He loves in John 17. For Jesus, prayer was backed up with actions. Go through John 17 again and list what Jesus does for those He loves and prays for.

_____

_____

_____

_____

_____

_____

_____

What do you need to adjust in your life to walk as Jesus walked in the area of prayer?

_____

_____

_____

FOR DEEPER REFLECTION

How does John 17 give you direction in praying for those you love?

What do the actions of Jesus in John 17 tell you about how you should act toward those you love? Be very practical and specific.

Has this week's study changed your view of Jesus? If so, how?

WEEKS 1–4 SUMMARY

1. Jesus is our model for life and ministry and we are commanded to "walk as He walked."

2. In His humanity, Jesus was man as God intended mankind to be, showing us how to walk.

3. The first foundational priority we see in Jesus' humanity was total dependence on the Holy Spirit in everything He did.

4. The second priority we see is how Jesus "often slipped away to pray." He lived a life of prayerful guidance.

OBEYING AS JESUS OBEYED

See WalkingAsJesus.com for video resources specific to this week's study.

GETTING STARTED

'm writing this unit in a cabin in the Galena Territory of northern Illinois and listening to a song by Darrell Evans titled "Trading my Sorrows." The chorus captures the essence of one foundational priority in Jesus' life:

> I'm trading my sorrows; I'm trading my shame;
> I'm laying them down for the joy of the Lord.
> And we say, "Yes, Lord; Yes, Lord; Yes, Yes, Lord."[1]

"Yes" is the word of obedience. And obedience is God's love language! Jesus always and only obeyed His Father's desires. Jesus always and only said, "Yes, Father; not My will but Yours be done." What an amazing thought! What a challenging example.

It's amazing to me that when Jesus became flesh and dwelt among us, He did not live according to His own desires. Instead, He entered into His Father's plan for all of creation and mankind. Jesus didn't come preaching "My Kingdom come," but "Thy Kingdom come!"

For over thirty years, Jesus lived a relatively obscure life of quiet obedience to His Father. When Jesus finally began His ministry, He labored for several months in the shadow of John the Baptist, whom God sent "to prepare the way." Jesus' obedience meant that He entered into His Father's kingdom agenda. Jesus knew that His Father was writing a metanarrative, and He willingly entered into that grand story and fulfilled His role as the lead character.

Jesus made it clear that He only did what pleased His Father (John 8:29). In the same way, we are to "find out what pleases the Lord" (Ephesians 5:10). Jesus clearly understood what it takes so long for many of us to discover. Jesus knew that His Father was weaving a beautiful story of creation, redemption, and re-creation, and He had chosen men and women to play a major part in His kingdom agenda. Beauty and glory are realized when we willingly and obediently submit to the Father's agenda and find our place in the kingdom story.

As we discussed in a previous unit, Jesus did what Adam could not do. Any movement outside of the Father's agenda is called "sin." Adam sinned when he failed to fulfill his role in creation by eating from the forbidden tree. Jesus, on the other hand, never stepped outside of God's plan. He was sinless. He always and only did His Father's will, preaching that the kingdom of God had come near and calling others to enter into that kingdom agenda (John 3:5).

Jesus knew that the question was not, "What do I want to do?" but, "What does My Father want Me to do?" Jesus knew that life presents two choices. We can follow either the world's agenda, which involves living for ourselves; or we can choose to always and only follow the Father's kingdom agenda (John 5:30). For Jesus, the choice was clear. His life revolved not around His desires but around the Father's greater plan and story. Jesus willingly and sacrificially entered into that life of servanthood, and He called others to do the same.

In which arena have you lived most of your earthly life? Make an honest assessment of your obedience on the scale of 1–10 below.

1	2	3	4	5	6	7	8	9	10

Living always and
only for yourself

Living always and only for
kingdom agenda

FOR DEEPER REFLECTION

Read John 8:29 aloud. Then write out the verse in your own words.

For you, what is the most difficult part of trying to please the Lord? Spend some time in prayer. Tell the Lord honestly what you are thinking.

Obedience and His Birth DAY 1

Throughout the Old Testament there are numerous examples of halfhearted obedience. The trouble is, partial obedience is disobedience. One of the most graphic examples of partial obedience in the Old Testament is Saul's failure to follow the Lord's command in 1 Samuel 15. What did God command Saul to do in verses 1–3?

_____

_____

_____

How did Saul respond? (verses 7–9)

_____

_____

_____

How did God respond to Saul? (verses 10–11)

_____

_____

_____

How did Saul try to justify his actions? (verses 12–21)

_____

_____

_____

What is Samuel's final word on the matter? (verses 22–23)

_____

_____

_____

Philippians 2 opens the window into eternity past and lets us see a glimpse of what happened when Christ became flesh and dwelt among us. The passage begins with the exhortation that our "attitude should be the same as that of Christ Jesus"; or as the NCV translates the Greek, "In your lives you must think and act like Christ Jesus" (2:5). At the end of the passage, Paul makes this appeal: "My dear friends, as you have always obeyed . . . continue to work out your salvation with fear and trembling, for it is God who works in you to will and to act according to his good purpose" (2:12–13).

> He has the right to interrupt your life. He is Lord. When you accepted Him as Lord, you gave Him the right to help Himself to your life anytime He wants.
>
> —Henry Blackaby

Between these two challenges to imitate the obedience of Jesus, Paul breaks down just what Jesus' obedience involved. Philippians 2:6–7 tells us that Jesus, though "being in very nature (*morphe*) God," Jesus "did not consider equality with God something to be grasped, but made himself nothing, taking the very nature (*morphe*) of a servant, being made in human likeness." Jesus willingly humbled Himself by becoming flesh, a human baby born into a poor family in the Middle East. This meant leaving the glory of heaven to enter this sinful world. But that's not all. Jesus' obedience took Him even further. For Paul tells us, "being found in appearance as a man, he humbled himself by becoming obedient to death—even death on a cross!" (verse 8). Not only was Jesus obedient enough to become part of the sinful world, He was even obedient enough to die a sinner's death on the cross.

How would you contrast the obedience of Saul with the obedience of Jesus?

Saul's obedience   Jesus' obedience

_____
_____
_____

Based on Christ's example, what does complete obedience look like?

_____
_____
_____

Like Jesus, what will complete obedience ultimately require of us? (See Matthew 16:24–26.)

_____
_____
_____

FOR DEEPER REFLECTION

Why is it sometimes so difficult to be fully obedient? Be specific.

Based on your study above, what needs to change in your life so that you better reflect Christ's obedience?

DAY 2 Obedience as a Young Boy

Every parent knows the challenge of training their children to be obedient. I have three daughters, and I remember my oldest daughter as a strong-willed four-year-old saying, "I'll obey on the outside, but not on the inside!" Being told she was not to go outside of a gate, she would look back at us, smile, and then walk out of the gate in defiance. After being disciplined by Dad, she'd go back out into the yard, turn around, smile, and walk out the gate again, forcing another confrontation with Dad!

After multiple confrontations, and each becoming harder, my gentle wife was ready to call 911 to report child abuse. But as any parent knows, obedience cannot be in words alone. It must stem from the heart and result in proper action. Obedience must be learned. Our daughter has become a great joy . . . as she learned obedience. In the same way, obedience is God's love language.

Luke 2:41–52 provides our only canonical information about the childhood of Jesus, a snapshot of the twelve-year-old Messiah from which we can glean several helpful insights about the family of Jesus. Read this story. What does it tell us about Mary and Joseph?

_____

_____

_____

What does this story tell us about Jesus?

_____

_____

_____

How would you describe Jesus' response to His parents in Luke 2:51?

_____

_____

_____

This passage is the last time the Bible mentions Joseph. Many scholars believe that Joseph may have died when Jesus was young, perhaps shortly after this encounter in the temple. If this is true, how might this have affected Jesus? How might His life have changed?

_____

_____

_____

Hebrews 5:8 tells us that "Although he [Jesus] was a son, he learned obedience from what he suffered." Jesus suffered not only on the cross but as He lived life in perfect obedience to His Father throughout His life. Suffering is a part of life. Fortunately, Hebrews 2:18 tells us that "Because he himself suffered when he was tempted, he is able to help those who are being tempted." How does temptation bring suffering?

_____

_____

_____

What does Hebrews 11:25 tell us about sin?

_____

_____

_____

What happens in the short term when someone chooses to say no to the passing pleasure of sin (Hebrews 2:18)? What is the long-term result (Hebrews 12:2)?

_____

_____

_____

With these verses in mind, write down what you think it means that Jesus "learned obedience by what he suffered."

_____

_____

_____

WALKING AS JESUS WALKED

FOR DEEPER REFLECTION

What do you think it means that Jesus "learned obedience" (reread Hebrews 5)?

There are two ways to learn obedience: through disobedience (sin) or through obedience. How do the lessons differ?

Obedience as a Young Man DAY 3

As I mentioned in the previous lesson, Luke 2 gives us our only peek into Jesus' childhood. We don't know what happened in the first twelve years of His life. But Luke 2:51 gives us a one-sentence summary of the next eighteen years of Jesus' life. We might wish we knew more. But this verse tells us quite a bit. Read Luke 2:51–52. What does it tell you about the young man Jesus?

_____

_____

_____

The years between the time in the temple and the beginning of Jesus' public ministry are often called the "silent years." We assume that Jesus continued to work as a *tekton* (carpenter or stonecutter), learning the trade of his earthly father, Joseph. Since Nazareth was a small village of only a few hundred people, Jesus and Joseph may have made regular trips four miles away to work in Sepphoris, which was a booming town at the time. Herod was developing Sepphoris, a town of about 30,000 people, as a capital center for the region, complete with all the culture of a magnificent Roman capital city.

Let's stop for a moment to consider these years in Jesus' life. We know that He continued in sinless obedience both to His earthly parents and to His heavenly Father. If Joseph had indeed died while Jesus was still young, Jesus may have served as the leader and primary provider of His home. What might His relationship with His brothers and sisters have been like (Matthew 13:53–57)?

_____

_____

_____

How much did Jesus know about His calling and purpose as a young man? We know He had zeal for His Father's house and wanted to learn. Did He fully understand that He was the coming Messiah? In His humanity, did Jesus know everything automatically, or was His Father slowly revealing His plan to Jesus, as He so often does with you and me? Take a moment to write down what you think Jesus knew about His calling at this stage in His life.

_____

_____

_____

It seems safest to me to say that Jesus' heavenly Father gradually revealed His perfect plan to His Son. Jesus indicates this Himself in John 5:19–21. Spend a moment reflecting on this passage. What does it tell us about the Father's progressive revelation to His Son?

_____

_____

_____

It is difficult for me to believe that Jesus always knew His Father's complete plan for His life. Scripture indicates on several occasions that Jesus "learned" (John 15:15) and was "being taught" (John 12:49) and in His youth was "growing in wisdom and stature" (Luke 2:52). Because Jesus was fully human, I believe the Father gradually and perfectly revealed His plan to His Son through prayer, the Scriptures, and the Holy Spirit. This position does not diminish the uniqueness of Jesus or His deity. Instead, it exalts what He did for us! It demonstrates the depth of His love for us as He "made Himself nothing, taking the very nature of a servant, being made in human likeness" (Philippians 2:7). He became "like us in every way" to show us the way to live life.

> The true follower of Christ will not ask, "If I embrace this truth, what will it cost me?" Rather he will say, "This is truth. God help me to walk in it, let come what may!"
>
> —A. W. Tozer

With this perspective in mind, try to creatively imagine the morning when the Father said to Jesus, "Today is the day. Go with me on an eighty-mile journey out of Nazareth to Bethany, to the other side of the Jordan. There you will find your cousin, John, baptizing your countrymen for repentance. Go and be baptized by him." Read the biblical account of this event in John 1:29–34. How did John know Jesus was the one He was preaching about?

_____

_____

_____

It took great obedience on John's part to preach that the Messiah was coming, when he didn't know who the Messiah was or when He would arrive. Likewise, it took complete obedience on Jesus' part to trust in His Father's perfect timing. Matthew 3:13–17 speaks of John's humility and gives us another version of these events. It also speaks of Jesus' complete submission to His Father's perfect plan. How does the Father respond to Jesus' obedience?

_____

_____

_____

Obedience is indeed God's love language!

Describe a time when God asked you to step out in bold obedience to Him.

_____

_____

_____

FOR DEEPER REFLECTION

Do you think Jesus always knew He was the Messiah? What light does John 5:19–20 and John 15:15 shed on this question?

Did John the Baptist know who the Messiah was? (See John 1:32–33.) Why do you think John might have been unsure? Wouldn't his mother, Elizabeth, have explained it to him?

DAY 4 Obedience and Suffering

Jesus' public ministry was the next phase in His Father's plan. When He accepted this plan for His life, Jesus continued his lifestyle of "reverent submission" (Hebrews 5:7). Read the following passages. How does Jesus describe His own obedience?

John 5:19

_____
_____
_____

John 5:30

_____
_____
_____

John 8:29

_____
_____
_____

John 14:31

_____
_____
_____

The obedience that Jesus practiced rarely resulted in prosperity, comfort, or self-centered pleasure. In fact, Jesus' obedience can be characterized primarily as service to others and self-sacrifice. What do the following verses have to say about the nature of Jesus' obedience?

John 10:17 and Matthew 16:21

_____

_____

_____

Matthew 26:37–39

_____

_____

_____

John 13:14–15

_____

_____

_____

Philippians 2 tells us that Jesus obeyed His Father's will all the way to the cross. His was a life of perfect obedience to His Father's agenda. What does this say about our calling?

_____

_____

_____

FOR DEEPER REFLECTION

What did you discover in this lesson about "how" Jesus obeyed? Give examples from the Bible verses above.

Read Hebrews 11:32–39. What did the saints of old receive as a result of their obedience?

DAY 5 Obedience and the Everyday Commission

Jesus' parting words to His disciples in Matthew 28:16–20 are known today as the Great Commission. In this final lesson, Jesus tells His disciples—and us again today—to do what He did, to walk as He walked, by making disciples who can make disciples. "All authority in heaven and on earth has been given to me," He said. "Therefore go and make disciples of all nations, baptizing them in the name of the Father and of the Son and of the Holy Spirit, and teaching them to obey everything I have commanded you. And surely I am with you always, to the very end of the age."

In these concise words, Jesus summarizes His life and leaves us with His parting challenge to follow His example. Notice how Jesus emphasizes that we are to teach obedience. Some have stated that simply teaching is the Great Omission. The Great Commission involves teaching *to obey*! Jesus gave approximately 405 commands in his lifetime, and He charges us to teach "everything I have commanded you." How does "teaching to obey" differ from just teaching? Think about it and make your list.

> If a commission by an earthly king is considered an honour, how can a commission by a Heavenly King be considered a sacrifice?
>
> —David Livingstone

Teaching	Teaching to obey

Parents know that teaching their children to obey is crucial. If you are a parent, why is it important that your children learn how to obey you? Or if you aren't a parent, why is obedience critical in any aspect of life? Write some of the reasons below.

What practical steps can you take to elevate obedience as a greater priority in your life?

_____

_____

_____

We will never become sinless, but we should sin less. How long do you think it is possible to live without any known sin in your life? (See 1 John 1:9.) Explain your answer.

_____

_____

_____

If we do sin, what is the very next step of obedience that the Lord commands us to take? (See 1 John 1:9.)

_____

_____

_____

FOR DEEPER REFLECTION

How are children taught to obey? What lessons can we learn from this about how God teaches us obedience?

Was obedience easier for Jesus when He was young? Did it become more difficult as He grew older? Why or why not?

WEEKS 1-5 SUMMARY

Presently we are halfway through this study. In review, we have concluded the following about "walking as Jesus walked."

1. Jesus is our model for life and ministry and we are commanded to "walk as He walked."

2. In His humanity, Jesus was man as God intended mankind to be, showing us how to walk.

3. The first foundational priority we see in Jesus' humanity was total dependence on the Holy Spirit in everything He did.

4. The second priority we see is how Jesus "often slipped away to pray." He lived a life of prayerful guidance.

5. Third, out of reverent submission, Jesus learned obedience and calls us to that same lifestyle of obedience.

In the next part, we will look at Jesus' attitude toward the Scriptures.

JESUS AND THE WORD OF GOD

See WalkingAsJesus.com for video resources specific to this week's study.

GETTING STARTED

As we continue to learn to walk as Jesus walked, we must now turn our attention to Jesus' attitude toward the Word of God. If we want to model our lives after Jesus' example, as He calls us to do, then we must hold the same view of Scripture He did. So how did Jesus approach God's Word? How did He relate to Scripture?

As we begin to seek the "mind of Christ" (1 Corinthians 2:16) in this area, one thing is clear. Jesus never made light of Scripture. Never did He downplay the significance of Scripture for His personal guidance, nor did He doubt the authority of God's Word, question the Old Testament stories, or challenge their veracity.

On the contrary, Jesus held the Bible in the highest esteem. Eighty times in the Gospels Jesus quotes from more than seventy chapters from twenty-four different Old Testament books. The Word was center stage in Jesus' life and ministry. The Scriptures formed the basis of His rebuke of other religious leaders. He accused the Sadducees of ignorance, claiming, "You are in error because you don't know the Scriptures" (Matthew 22:29). He asks His opponents over and over, "Have you never read?" (Matthew 21:16, 21:42; 22:31). The Scriptures were His defense against the temptations of Satan.

Jesus knew the Scriptures thoroughly, even down to the verb tenses and smallest of words. He warned against supplanting the authority of the Word with manmade traditions. He lived His life in submission to what was written about Him in the Word. Jesus' respect for, knowledge of, and dependence on the Word of God are evident at every turn in His life.

So let's begin this week by reflecting on what Jesus Himself had to say about the Bible. Turn to Matthew 5:17–19.

According to verse 17, how did Christ see His role?

_____

_____

_____

Jesus recognized that His life was a fulfillment of the words of the Law and Prophets. Imagine how you would respond if you understood your life in the same way. Imagine how carefully you would study the Scriptures if you felt your job was to fully obey all that was written in it. Imagine how diligently you would examine the Bible if you truly believed it contained your assignments for life. This was Jesus' attitude. His passion was knowing and living out the written Word. He did not want to "turn from it to the right or to the left" but "to be careful to do everything written in it" (Joshua 1:7–8).

What does Matthew 5:18 tell us about Jesus' respect for and confidence in the written Word of God?

_____

_____

_____

The word used here is *yod*, the name of the smallest letter in the Hebrew alphabet. The Greek word translated the "least stroke of a pen" here literally means "a little horn," "a point," or "an extremity." (You might be familiar with the "jot and tittle" wording from the King James Version.) Several Hebrew letters were written with small points that distinguished one letter from another. Changing a small point of one letter, therefore, might vary the meaning of a word completely. When Jesus said, "Not one jot or tittle shall pass from the Law," He was referring to these tiny marks. For Jesus, all of Scripture, even the smallest pen strokes, demanded His total allegiance and obedience.

What two attitudes toward God's Word does Jesus present in Matthew 5:19? How do these attitudes differ?

_____

_____

_____

Jesus' attitude toward the written Word of God was careful submission and obedience to every part of it. This should be our attitude too, as we strive to walk as Jesus walked.

FOR DEEPER REFLECTION

In your own words, what does Matthew 5:17–19 tell us about Jesus' attitude toward Scripture?

If you are to "think and act" just like Jesus, is there anything in your attitude toward the Scriptures that needs to change?

DAY 1 Jesus Studied the Scriptures

Some people are quick to assume that, because Jesus was fully God, from the time He was a little baby He was downloaded with all the important biblical data. As if He had access to a cosmic software update, many assume that all Jesus had to do was to press a button to instantly receive a perfect understanding of God's Word. It should be clear by now at this point in our study that Scripture gives a very different perspective.

In the first century, when Jesus lived on earth, all Jewish boys studied God's Word. The smartest students would memorize all of the Torah (the first five books of the Bible) by age twelve. Rabbis tested them by quoting a verse and asking the student to quote the verses before and after it.

Perhaps we can assume that Jesus was particularly gifted in memory, because He did not have a fallen intellect as we do. We cannot assume, however, that He never had to study, or that He was born with an innate knowledge of the Bible.

Read Luke 2:40. What does this verse tell us about Jesus' intellectual development? How did Jesus get wisdom?

_____

_____

_____

Now read Luke 2:52. How are 2:40 and 2:52 similar? What do they communicate that's different?

_____

_____

_____

Look closely at Luke 2:41–47. What was Jesus doing for three days in the temple courts at the age of twelve? Don't assume too quickly that Jesus was lecturing the teachers. The text communicates something different. What does this episode tell us about Jesus' love of the Word and desire to learn?

_____

_____

_____

After beginning His ministry at about the age of thirty, we find Jesus a second time in His hometown of Nazareth (Luke 4:16). What does this passage tell us about the habits of Jesus in His hometown?

_____

_____

_____

Jesus demonstrates His careful grasp of the Word in this situation. He stops reading when He comes to the part about "the year of the Lord's favor." This is a clear reference to the Lord's first advent and the gracious offering of Himself (Genesis 3:15; Acts 1:11). But the very next verse speaks of the second coming, "the day of vengeance of our God" (Isaiah 61:2b). Jesus clearly understood how the details of Scripture applied to His life. He grasped His identity and His Father's will for Him through a careful study of the Word.

In the same way, we need to learn about our identity in Christ through the careful study of God's Word. What are some of the things God's Word tells us about our identity? Where would you go in Scripture to learn about your identity in Christ?

_____

_____

_____

FOR DEEPER REFLECTION

How did the people in Jesus' hometown react to His grasp of Scripture? (See Matthew 13:53–57.)

In the space below, summarize what you have learned about Jesus' attitude toward the Scriptures.

> **Dusty Bibles always lead to dirty lives. In fact, you are either in the Word and the Word is conforming you to the image of Jesus Christ, or you are in the world and the world is squeezing you into its mold.**
>
> **—Howard G. Hendricks**

DAY 2 Jesus Trusted the Scriptures

Not once did Jesus question the truth of the Scriptures. Jesus viewed reality through the conviction that the Old Testament Scriptures were true. Jesus began with the assumption that the Bible is God's Word, and He allowed it to speak for itself.

Today we want to consider what Jesus assumes to be true based on the testimony of the Old Testament.

What book does Jesus quote from in Matthew 19:4–5? What does He claim is accurate?

_____

_____

_____

According to Matthew 22:31–32, who spoke through the Old Testament? Who did Jesus consider to be the author of the Scripture?

_____

_____

_____

Who does Jesus say spoke through David in Matthew 22:43? Do you think Jesus questioned whether David was a historical figure?

_____

_____

_____

Below are a number of other historical individuals and events that Jesus trusted were true because of His view of Scripture. List them:

Matthew 8:11

_____

_____

_____

Matthew 10:15; 11:23—24

_____

_____

_____

Matthew 12:39—41

_____

_____

_____

Matthew 24:15

_____

_____

_____

Matthew 24:37—39

_____

_____

_____

Luke 11:51

_____

_____

_____

John 3:14

_____

_____

_____

John 8:56—58

_____

_____

_____

Jesus trusted and respected the Word of God. He believed that God the Father had recorded His words accurately and for our instruction. If we are to walk as Jesus walked, how should we view Scripture?

_____

_____

_____

FOR DEEPER REFLECTION

How did Jesus' view of the Scriptures differ from that of the liberalism of the Sadducees or the legalism of the Pharisees?

How might your worldview change if you fully approached Scripture the way Jesus did?

Jesus Learned from the Scriptures DAY 3

All of us are shaped by certain influences. Our perception of reality and approach to life is shaped by where we learn our life lessons. Every parent is deeply concerned about what influences shape a child's life. Jesus, in His humanity, was no different. He was a student who "grew in wisdom and stature and in favor with God and men" (Luke 2:52).

Jesus drew His understanding of reality from His Father's Word. He was a diligent student of Scripture. He understood that to see and interpret reality accurately, He must have a clear understanding of His Father's plan. Over seventy-five times in the Gospels, Jesus says, "I tell you the truth" (Matthew 8:10, and 10:15 for example). Reality was rooted in the truth. For Jesus, Scripture was that truth.

Look at John 7:16–17. Where does Jesus say that His teaching comes from?

_____

_____

_____

What does this say to us about how Jesus learned?

_____

_____

_____

Jesus makes even stronger statements about the role of Scripture in both His learning and teaching when He said, "I do nothing on my own but speak just as the Father has taught me" (John 8:28). What does this tell us about Jesus and His humanity?

_____

_____

_____

For some years now I have read through the Bible twice every year. If you picture the Bible to be a mighty tree and every word a little branch, I have shaken every one of these branches because I wanted to know what it was and what it meant.

—Martin Luther

If Jesus could only say what His Father had taught Him, and if Jesus could do nothing of His own accord, what does this tell us about ourselves? (Hint: see John 15:5b.)

_____

_____

_____

Look up the following verses to see how the truly human Jesus was a student of His Father's Word. Record your thoughts and insights in the spaces provided below.

John 12:49

_____

_____

_____

To whom do the words of Scripture belong? (John 14:24)

_____

_____

_____

How, then, should we approach learning God's Word? (John 14:26)

_____

_____

_____

What does Jesus promise to reveal to us? Where did Jesus receive what He will make known to us? (John 15:15)

_____

_____

_____

Jesus was a student of His Father's Word. Jesus knew the perfect will of His Father because He submitted to the Word of God through the Spirit of God, and remained a man of prayer. Jesus humbly acknowledged His Father as the source of all truth. This is the example we are to follow.

As we have said before, Jesus was man as God intended man to be. Part of what it means to be fully human is to be a student of the Word. This is the only way our words can be His words, our thoughts His thoughts, our teaching grounded in the truth that comes from God.

FOR DEEPER REFLECTION

Write out carefully below the one verse in this lesson that made the greatest impact on you. What was it about this verse that made it so significant for you?

Summarize below what you have learned from these verses about Jesus' attitude toward the Scriptures.

DAY 4 Jesus Submitted to the Scriptures

John 1:1–2 gives us the clearest statement about Jesus' deity in all the Gospels: "In the beginning was the Word," John exclaims, "and the Word was with God, and the Word was God. He was with God in the beginning." Not only was Jesus devoted to the Word of God, Jesus *was* the Word of God. He was the living Word (*logos*) who chose to become a servant to the written Word.

Because Jesus is the living Word of God, He could have written new rules for His life and ministry. He could have exerted His authority as God and spoken anything into reality. But in His humanity He modeled something very different for us. He humbled Himself and chose to live in submission to the written Word of God. He subjected Himself to the Scriptures. They became His authority.

Today we want to explore how Jesus lived according to the written Word of God, how He modeled for us the way to find God's direct will in the Scriptures. Write out and reflect on the following verses in the spaces provided.

Through the Word, Jesus understood His destiny (Matthew 26:24a).

_____

_____

_____

Through the Word, Jesus understood how to respond to His Father's plan for Him (Matthew 26:54).

_____

_____

_____

Through the Word, Jesus understood how His life was going to unfold (Matthew 26:56).

_____

_____

_____

Through the Word, Jesus understood what to expect from life (Mark 9:12).

_____

_____

_____

Through the Word, Jesus understood His mission (Luke 4:18–19; 18:31–33).

_____

_____

_____

Through the Word, Jesus understood when things would happen (Luke 22:37).

_____

_____

_____

Through the Word, Jesus came to understand who He was, what His role was, and how He was to live (Luke 24:25–27, 44).

_____

_____

_____

Where do we learn about our true identity, our mission, our calling, and our destiny? The Word of God is living and active. Could it be that God is able to lead us into all truth through His Word, just as He did with Jesus?

FOR DEEPER REFLECTION

What do the Scriptures tell us about our:

> *Identity:*
>
> *Mission:*
>
> *What is my unique calling? That is, what is my part in furthering God's kingdom?*

What barriers keep us from understanding from the Word our identity, our mission, and our unique calling?

DAY 5 Jesus Used the Scriptures

One of the characteristics of Jesus is that He used the Scriptures for guidance in everyday life situations. The many different ways and situations in which Jesus used the Scriptures speak volumes about His comprehensive grasp of Scripture. As Jesus went through daily life, we find Him using Scripture as He approached everyday life events.

Today we will examine some of the ways Jesus used the Scriptures. As you read and reflect on the passages below, list the different ways Jesus used the Word. Then think about application. How do these passages apply to you as you seek to use the Scriptures as Jesus used the Scriptures, living a fully human lifestyle?

> I seek the will of the Spirit of God through, or in connection with, the Word of God. The Spirit and the Word must be combined. If I look to the Spirit alone without the Word, I lay myself open to great delusions. If the Holy Spirit leads us, He will do it according to the Scriptures and never contrary to them.
>
> —George Mueller

How Jesus used Scripture	How we are to use Scripture
Matthew 4:4	James 4:7
Matthew 19:3–6	2 Timothy 2:25–26
Mark 1:21–22	2 Timothy 2:15–16

Luke 4:18–19   Psalm 119:35–37

_____

_____

_____

Luke 4:25–27   Hebrews 4:12

_____

_____

_____

Hebrews 5:5–8   Psalm 119:71

_____

_____

_____

Learning to walk as Jesus walked requires that we understand how Jesus approached the Scriptures. As we have seen, Jesus studied and learned from the Word. He respected the Word. He submitted to and used the Word in His everyday decisions. Every aspect of Jesus' life on earth was saturated with God's love letter to us—His written Word. To be fully human like Jesus demands that we submit to and hunger for God's Word with "reverent submission." Jesus, the true man, models the attitude toward Scripture that we are to emulate!

FOR DEEPER REFLECTION

What keeps us from being Word-centered like Jesus?

What aspect of this unit was most challenging for you?

> One of the many divine qualities of the Bible is that it does not yield its secrets to the irreverent and the censorious.
>
> **—James I. Packer**

From memory, can you state the first four priorities in Jesus' life? (Hint: Use the acronym Holy Spirit POWER.)

WEEKS 1–6 SUMMARY

1. Jesus is our model for life and ministry and we are commanded to "walk as He walked."

2. In His humanity, Jesus was man as God intended mankind to be, showing us how to walk.

3. The first foundational priority we see in Jesus' humanity was total dependence on the Holy Spirit in everything He did.

4. The second priority we see is how Jesus "often slipped away to pray." He lived a life of prayerful guidance.

5. Third, out of reverent submission, Jesus learned obedience and calls us to that same lifestyle of obedience.

6. Fourth, Jesus trusted, studied, learned from, and submitted to the Scriptures. He used the Scriptures as He approached the demands of living a holy life. He was Word-centered.

EXALTING THE FATHER

See WalkingAsJesus.com for video resources specific to this week's study.

GETTING STARTED

What would it be like to be like Adam and Eve before they sinned? How did they think and act? What was their attitude like? Write down some initial thoughts:

_____

_____

_____

Genesis tells us that they had the perfect relationship, the perfect job, and lived in a perfectly beautiful world. Every day they literally had devotions with God Himself, in person, as they walked in the cool of the day in the garden. There was no selfishness, no greed, and no ingratitude. There was no pain, no sorrow, and no tears. Living without a sinful nature in a sinless world would have been an incredible experience.

Remarkably, this will be the destiny of Christ-followers. We will one day live life totally free from the curse of sin.

This, however, is not our present reality. Because we have always lived in a sinful world, with a sinful nature, we find it hard to imagine life before or after the curse of sin. Thankfully though, through the record of Scriptures, we see Jesus as the second Adam, living without sin in our present world. Not only did He die for our sins as the sacrificial Lamb of God, but He became our model for life the way God wanted us to live.

Jesus lived His life without sinning. He was man as God intended man to be. He modeled what full humanity should be like, experiencing life "to the full" (John 10:10). He lived in a sinful world, and yet never gave in to sin. At times He wept, other times He became angry, yet without sin. His worldview was shaped by the Word of God. His daily actions were guided by the Spirit of God. He lived in perfect communion with the Father. He saw others perfectly and His heart was full of the Father's love. He lived in perfect humility, always in a posture of complete dependence and gratefulness to His Father. He did what Adam failed to do . . . He always and only obeyed with the perfect attitude and actions. And then we are told to have that same attitude . . . to "think and act" just like Jesus (Philippians 2:5 NCV).

So far in this study we have identified that Jesus, in His humanity, is the model of how we are to live our lives since He commanded us to "walk as He walked." We have identified priorities of Jesus in His humanity. First was full dependence on the Spirit of God. Second, we observed His prayerful lifestyle. Third, we studied how He learned obedience and always lived to please His Father. Fourth, we have just observed how Jesus centered His life on the Word . . . studying, using, honoring, and submitting His life to the centrality of God's Word and its fulfillment in His life.

In this unit, we want to explore another priority in the life and ministry of this fully human Jesus—a priority He clearly modeled in every aspect of His life.

Early in His ministry, Jesus offers a clear statement about what this priority looks like and what full humanity looks like. His words have the power to transform, if we have ears to hear them clearly.

In John 3:21, Jesus establishes a principle to all who will follow Him, giving us a glimpse of His attitude when He says: "Whoever lives by the truth comes into the light, so that it may be seen plainly that what he has done has been done through God."

Read this verse in your Bible. Jot down your first impressions about what it is saying.

_____

_____

_____

Jesus communicates to Nicodemus that living by the truth and walking in the light causes us to acknowledge that any good in our life is a result of God working through us! And then He powerfully states that the more we walk in truth, the more we see "plainly" that "what he has done has been done through God."

Isaiah 26:12b makes this same point in a slightly different way. It says, ". . . all that we have accomplished you have done for us." Jesus clearly modeled this attitude of true humility. He often stated that by Himself He could do nothing (see John 5:19).

This is a clear picture of biblical humility, a picture of what it means to be fully human. We are called to live a lifestyle of total dependence on God, as a vessel through whom He chooses to flow. Living as Jesus lived means always and only acknowledging the Father as the source of all. This liberating reality will be the focus of this week's study.

FOR DEEPER REFLECTION

John 3:19–20 presents an alternative to John 3:21. What alternative do people have to living in darkness?

What would it mean to live daily with John 3:21 as your mind-set? How would this affect your lifestyle?

DAY 1 The Principle Expanded

Jesus makes it very clear that walking in the light causes us to plainly see that whatever good we do is the work of God through us. Jesus lived with this awareness and always and only exalted His Father as the source of everything. Since He always and only did good (Acts 10:38), He always and only acknowledged God as the source of that good. By the model of His life, we are to understand that this is what God intended it to look like to be "fully human."

I choose kindness. I will be kind to the poor, for they are alone. Kind to the rich, for they are afraid. And kind to the unkind, for such is how God has treated me.

—Max Lucado

Compare Isaiah 26:12 and the words Jesus spoke to Nicodemus as recorded in John 3:21. Who has done something—we or God? Is this concept inconsistent? Must it be one or the other? As you work through this concept, bear in mind that it is at the heart of how Jesus lived His life. And it should be at the heart of ours too, as we learn to walk as Jesus walked.

Turn in your Bible to John 17:7. Jesus prayed this prayer at the very end of His life. Pay close attention to what Jesus is saying. What does He say about His disciples?

_____

_____

_____

How much did Jesus say came from the Father? Jesus could have said that "most things" come from above. Why do you think He didn't say this?

_____

_____

_____

At the beginning of His ministry (John 3:21) and again at the end (John 17:7), Jesus made it clear that being fully human means that we are to be clean vessels through whom God can work. It means recognizing that God is the source of all good things, and men and women are the vehicles God fills for His service. This is why Jesus said "I have brought you glory" (John 17:4). This is a lifestyle of exalting the Father . . . a lifestyle of honest humility. How do you see this principle of humility stated in the following verses?

John 5:19

_____

_____

_____

John 5:30

_____

_____

_____

John 8:28

_____

_____

_____

John 10:32

_____

_____

_____

John 12:49–50

_____

_____

_____

John 15:15

_____

_____

_____

Every aspect of Jesus' life exalted the Father. Many would like to call this biblical worship, but I have resisted doing this because the moment we say "worship" many think of a Sunday morning time of singing. Biblical worship is always and only exalting the Lord as the source of everything.

What happens in our life when we begin to see plainly that our heavenly Father is the source of everything good that we have and do?

_____

_____

_____

FOR DEEPER REFLECTION

Which of the verses above has the greatest impact on you? Write it out word for word below and underline what you feel are the key words.

Jesus lived the opposite of the downward progression you see unfolding in Romans 1:18–32. What does this passage tell us about what happens when we fail to acknowledge God as the source of everything?

The Pattern Lived Out DAY 2

Genuine humility, which is a by-product of understanding the Lord as the source of everything, produces great peace. This is why in Isaiah 26:12 Isaiah writes, "Lord, you establish peace for us."

Peace does not come from having an abundance of resources. Rather, peace comes when, in full humility, we acknowledge God as the source of all that we have and are. This is the peace that "transcends all understanding" (Philippians 4:6), for it comes not from striving, but from resting in the goodness and grace of our heavenly Father.

Read John 7:16–18. Jesus is exalting His Father by acknowledging, "My teaching is not my own. It comes from him who sent me." He continues by drawing a principle from His conduct in verse 18: "He who speaks on his own does so to gain honor for himself, but he who works for the honor of the one who sent him is a man of truth; there is nothing false about him."

What happens when we strive to gain honor for ourselves? (Think this through carefully.)

_____

_____

_____

What happens when we work for the honor of someone else? (Think this through carefully.)

_____

_____

_____

Jesus did not say that life revolves around His own desires . . . it was about the Father and His desires. In the same way, life is not about me, nor does the world revolve around my desires. But when I make it all about me, then I feel pressure to live up to other people's expectations, or I measure myself against others. Life becomes about my performance—or lack of it. If I fail to meet my own or others' expectations, I become discouraged and wear myself out trying to perform as well as I feel I should.

In short, I'm so focused on myself that my goal becomes to indirectly bring glory to myself.

When, by contrast, we exalt the Father as the source of all the good we do, we live in genuine humility and peace comes our way. It is not about us, but about Him. This is how Jesus lived. The goal of His life was not about securing glory for Himself, but glorifying His heavenly Father (John 17:4).

Jesus lived by this principle. He stated in John 5:30, "I seek not to please myself but him who sent me" and in John 8:29, "The one who has sent me is with me; he has not left me alone, for I always do what pleases him." Being fully human means to live in the freedom of always and only pleasing the one who sent us. Exalting the Father as the source of everything is making life all about Him.

Why is genuine humility a by-product of exalting the Father? Explain what genuine humility looks and feels like in your life.

_____

_____

_____

What happens to our attitude when we fail to exalt the Father?

_____

_____

_____

FOR DEEPER REFLECTION

Reread John 7:16–18. What does this passage mean to you?

What application do these verses have for your life right now?

Our Position in Christ DAY 3

Last time we discussed how, throughout His life and ministry, Jesus always exalted His Father as the source of everything He did. This type of lifestyle brings freedom and joy, for it shifts the focus away from our own glory and performance and onto God and what He is doing in the world.

Once I considered this perspective, I began to compare my life with Christ's. I found that in contrast to what Christ did, I was spending most of my time telling people what they should be *doing* for God. Jesus spent most of his time telling people *who He was*. My style was about doing-for-God, or performance-based Christianity, and Jesus' style was who-God-truly-is or grace-driven Christianity. During the first two and a half years of His ministry, Jesus taught His disciples who God was, what He was doing for them, and who they were in Him. Only when they began to understand these things did He begin to tell them what they should do for Him.

The apostle Paul demonstrates the same pattern in his writings. Paul begins all of his letters with the indicative mood (which describe how things are) and then shifts later to the imperative mood (commands that describe how people should behave). In other words, each of his letters follows the same pattern of Jesus. He begins by describing what it means to be *in* Christ before he commands them to do anything *for* Christ.

For example, in Ephesians 1–3 Paul lists some thirty things God has done for us in Christ before he begins to emphasize how we should behave in light of all that Christ has done for us. Paul calls this "living a life worthy of the calling we have received" (Ephesians 4:1). This pattern is repeated in all of Paul's writings.

Jesus clearly understood this principle. He did not emphasize performing for God. Rather, He emphasized God's provision for us. Jesus knew that before His disciples could grasp doing things for God, they needed to understand who God is and what He had done for them. *Being* precedes *doing*. Grace precedes performance.

Colossians 2:6–7 restates this principle in this way: "So then, just as you received Christ Jesus

We don't serve God to gain His acceptance; we are accepted so we serve God. We don't follow Him in order to be loved; we are loved so we follow Him.

—Neil T. Anderson

as Lord (by faith alone) continue to live in him (with gratitude for what He has done for you), rooted and built up in him, strengthened in the faith as you were taught, and overflowing with thankfulness." According to this passage, how should our conduct be influenced when we fully grasp who God is and what He has done for us?

_____

_____

_____

Does your lifestyle model doing things for God because you *have* to or because you *want* to? What's the difference? Explain your response.

_____

_____

_____

Jesus clearly obeyed His Father's every desire not because He had to, but because He wanted to. Jesus fully understood and acknowledged His Father as the source of all good. Or as He put it in John 3:21, "Whoever lives by the truth comes into the light, so that it may be seen plainly that what he has done has been done through God." How does this attitude affect a person's life? Why did the disciples need to learn this truth?

_____

_____

_____

FOR DEEPER REFLECTION

Read Ephesians 1–3 and list all that God has done for you. How many things did you find? Why should realizing all that God has done for us produce genuine humility?

If you were to live today fully conscious of all that Christ has done for you, how would it change your day?

Our Performance versus Grace DAY 4

A number of years ago I had the privilege of leading a friend I'll call Tom to Christ. Tom was a very successful businessman, a top executive of a billion dollar company. He started coming to church because his wife had become a Christian and he liked the church—especially what it was doing for her. He attended for two years, although he had never made a decision for Christ himself. He felt that he didn't need Christ, but having faith was beneficial for his wife.

During that time, we became good friends. We had a lot in common. As a private pilot, I loved airplanes, and Tom had several Lear jets at his disposal. He was a farm boy from Iowa, and I was a farm boy from South Dakota. We bonded as only flying farmers can!

During a vacation at a lake together, I had the opportunity to share the gospel with Tom again. This time he listened not only with his head but also with his heart. When I challenged him to make this a day of decision, he went out to a large rock on the lake's edge and struggled with the Lord.

The next morning, Tom came to me and boldly said, "I did it!" I asked him what he meant and he explained that he had clearly seen his sin and trusted Christ alone for his salvation. We celebrated together as he shared with his family the decision he had made.

But in a follow-up conversation, I'll never forget what he said next.

"Now that I'm a new Christian, what do I need to do? I don't want to wimp out in following Christ," he said.

Chills went down my spine as I heard him make this statement. I would have been glad to hear this question from most new Christians, but Tom was different. He is very motivated and highly disciplined. I knew he would "do" whatever I told him to do. I was afraid that "after beginning with the Spirit," he would seek to attain his goal by "human effort" (Galatians 3:3).

As I looked at most of the follow-up material I had used with other new believers, I saw that it was primarily focused on telling them what they should "do" now that they were Christians. I knew I needed to proceed differently with Tom.

I happened to be working through a theology book at the time and was studying all that happens to us at the point of salvation.

So I said to Tom, "The Bible says that thirty-three things happened to you when you trusted Christ. Would you like to study those thirty-three things?"[1]

"I'd love to," Tom said. "When do you want to meet?"

"How about breakfast next Tuesday morning at seven?"

"I have to be at work at 7. How about 5:00?"

"Sure, no problem—I'll have been up for a couple of hours praying already," I said, joking.

We spent a whole hour talking about what it means to be a child of God . . . looking at the various verses in the Scriptures. After our first meeting, I asked Tom when he wanted to meet again and suggested next week.

"Why don't we meet twice a week?" he stated. "What about Thursday?"

"Sure. At 5 a.m.?" (I gulped but confirmed the time.)

As we met, we had a great time discovering what the Scriptures say about being totally forgiven of our sins.

After six weeks of meeting, I'll never forget what happened! At about 6:00 one morning, Tom took his Bible, slammed it shut, put it on the table and exclaimed loudly (causing everyone in the restaurant to look at us), "I can't stand it anymore! For six weeks *all* we have talked about is what God has done for me. Isn't there anything I can do for Him?"

I would be very happy to hear this from most new Christians, but as a highly driven and disciplined person, Tom was different. I quickly whispered a prayer to the Lord.

That morning I said something I'd never said before, but I've said many times since. "No, Tom, there is nothing you can do for Him. That is what grace is. God has done it all for you! And Tom, you will spend the rest of your life learning about that grace upon grace."

Tom is quite smart. I could see he was trying to comprehend this amazing grace, as true grace is so hard to comprehend.

After a while of letting him try to process this amazing truth, I replied, "Well, Tom, there is something you can do, but not because you *have* to. You do it because you *want* to!" I then began to go through all the "just as" verses in the Bible. "Just as God has forgiven you, you can forgive others. Just as God has loved you, you can love others. Just as God has served you, you can serve others. Just as God has given to you, you can give to me one of those Lear jets!" (It was worth a try!)

Tom's mind was spinning as he thought about this amazing concept. After a moment, he looked up and I'll never forget what he said—"Well, sign me up!"

In six short weeks, Tom moved from being a new believer to a biblical worker—one who works for God not because he *has* to, but because he *wants* to. He was one who plainly saw that all he has and does is from God above. Few grow so deep as quickly as Tom did. His life was rooted in who God is and what He has done for us. He clearly understood that all good that comes through his life is because of what God has done for and through him.

This is exactly what Jesus modeled: grace versus performance. Exalting the Father in every-thing. As Christ-followers, we have to ask: *Does the pattern of my life exalt the Lord in all things, or does it emphasize performance for God? Does my teaching exalt the Lord, focusing on who God is and what He has done for us, or is it about doing things for God? In our family, do our children see us exalting the Lord in everything that we have and do? Is the focus on Him or on me?* The beauty of this attitude that Jesus modeled is that it produces genuine peace rooted in true humility.

Turn to Ephesians 1–3 and list all the things the Lord has done for us. If you did this in the last lesson, take some time to reflect on what you wrote down. I started the list for you . . .

Ephesians 1:3   blessed us
1:4   chose us . . . made us holy and blameless

> In the greatest difficulties, in the heaviest trials, in the deepest poverty and necessities, He has never failed me; but because I was enabled by His grace to trust Him He has always appeared for my help. I delight in speaking well of His name.
>
> **—George Mueller**

1:5	predestined us . . . adopted us
1:6	has freely given us His grace . . . loves us
1:7	have redemption . . . forgiveness of sins
1:8	has lavished grace upon us
1:9	has made known His will
1:11	has chosen . . . predestined us
1:13	included us in Christ . . . saved us . . . marked us with the Holy Spirit . . . sealed us
1:14	guaranteed us an inheritance . . . redemption

_____

_____

_____

_____

_____

_____

_____

_____

_____

_____

A friend of mine always signs his letters with "Keep looking down for you are seated in the heavenly with Christ Jesus." A great attitude gained from thinking about who we are in Christ Jesus. The amazing truth about this principle is that when we begin to see that it is all about God and empty our egos from the equation, we are free to trust Him completely . . . allowing Him to work through us. We often underestimate what God wants to do through us, because we are consumed with an attitude that says we need to do it for God, versus acknowledging that it is all about what God wants to do through us!

FOR DEEPER REFLECTION

Which of the blessings above means the most to you? Pick one and write out your answer below.

Take time to praise the Lord for what He has done for you.

The Practice of Exalting the Lord DAY 5

Walking as Jesus walked demands thinking and acting like Jesus. Clearly Jesus understood the principle of exalting His Father as the source of everything. We have explored this throughout the week. He lived a lifestyle of worship, always humbly exalting His Father and helping others see that life was not about them, but about what God was doing in and through them. This was not burdensome for Jesus. It was His joy as He lived as a fully human being. It produced a peace that passed all human understanding as He faced the challenges of life.

So we would never forget this principle in our own lives, Jesus reminded His disciples in John 15 that "apart from me you can do nothing" (John 15:5). Just as in His humanity, Jesus acknowledged His dependence on the Father in everything; so He explains that we less-than-fully humans are dependent on Him for all things also. Read John 15. Why do you think Jesus brings this up in a conversation about bearing fruit? What was Jesus trying to help His disciples, and us, understand?

> Worship is not an optional extra, but is of the very life and essence of the Church. Man is never more truly man than when he exalts God.
>
> —James B. Torrance

_____

_____

_____

Did the disciples learn this principle? What does Jesus say in John 17:7? Why is this principle important for our disciples (or children or friends) to see in us?

_____

_____

_____

How does Peter exemplify this principle in Acts 3 (particularly verses 6, 12, and 16)?

_____

_____

_____

If you are married and have children, do your spouse or children recognize this principle at work in your life? If you lead a ministry, how can you communicate this principle to those you are investing in?

_____

_____

_____

FOR DEEPER REFLECTION

What changes do you need to make in your life so you can walk as Jesus walked on a daily basis?

Who do you know that best models the principle of always exalting the Father in their life? Describe them below and what this lifestyle looks like.

WEEKS 1–7 SUMMARY

1. Jesus is our model for life and ministry and we are commanded to "walk as He walked."

2. In His humanity, Jesus was man as God intended mankind to be, showing us how to walk.

3. The first foundational priority we see in Jesus' humanity was total dependence on the Holy Spirit in everything He did.

4. The second priority we see is how Jesus "often slipped away to pray." He lived a life of prayerful guidance.

5. Third, out of reverent submission, Jesus learned obedience and calls us to that same lifestyle of obedience.

6. Fourth, Jesus trusted, studied, learned from, and submitted to the Scriptures. He used the Scriptures as He approached the demands of living a holy life. He was Word-centered.

7. Fifth, Jesus always exalted His Father as the source of everything.

INTENTIONAL LOVING RELATIONSHIPS

See WalkingAsJesus.com for video resources specific to this week's study.

GETTING STARTED

In the next two sections we want to look at the sixth priority we have identified in Jesus' walk. So far we have looked at the following:

HS . . .	Holy Spirit dependence
P . . .	Prayerful guidance
O . . .	Obedient living
W . . .	Word-centered
E . . .	Exalting the Father

And now in the next two sections we want to look at the sixth priority, **R**= relational intentionality. We want to look at how Jesus was both a "friend" of sinners and a "friend" to His disciples.

Years ago, a friend of mine always used to say, "All change comes through relationships."

When I first heard this statement, I disagreed. But as I studied the life of Christ, I soon saw the reality of this principle in every aspect of Christ's life. Jesus' whole strategy of changing the world was rooted in building relationships with a few. As a matter of fact, the whole theology of the incarnation is that God became flesh and dwelt among us; Jesus adding humanity to His deity, to become one of us, to impart His life to us. Christ knew that life change happens through relationships!

The more I study the life of Jesus and the more I watch people's lives change, the more convinced I am that my friend was on the right path. Life change does come through relationships—whether it's a relationship between friends, between a parent and child, or a relationship with God through His Word. In fact, true Christianity is all about relationships, because full humanity means participating in and fostering loving relationships. Jesus was that true friend . . . both to sinners and His committed followers.

God's deep concern for genuine loving relationships is one of the reasons the Creator of the universe decided to become flesh and dwell among us. He wanted us to be sure we understood this truth. God did not just tell us that He loves us; He chose to show us His great love by walking with us in relationship. First John 4: 9–10 tells us that, "This is how God showed His love among us; He sent His one and only Son into the world that we might live through Him. This is love; not that we loved God, but that He loved us and sent His Son as an atoning sacrifice for our sins."

What amazes me about Jesus is that when He took on flesh to dwell among us, He did not come as a conquering king or even as a wealthy aristocrat. He came as a baby, born in a manger and raised in an obscure village called Nazareth for thirty years. He then spent the rest of His years investing in people.

Robert Coleman speaks powerfully about Jesus' relational focus on a few when he wrote:

> The multitudes of discordant and bewildered souls were potentially ready to follow Him, but Jesus individually could not possibly give them the personal care they needed. His only hope was to get men imbued with His life who would do it for Him. Hence, He concentrated Himself upon those who were to be the beginning of this leadership. Though He did what He could to help the multitudes, He had to devote Himself primarily to a few men, rather than the masses, in order that the masses could at last be saved. This was the genius of His strategy.[1]

It can often be said that people who are concentrating on a focused strategy often pursue their goals to the detriment of their relationships. *The remarkable thing about Jesus was that relationships were His strategy.*

Read John 1:14 and 1 John 4:9. How do these verses speak to God's commitment to having a relationship with His creatures?

_____

_____

_____

In his excellent book *The Fisherman*, Larry Huntsperger presents a fictional story of how Peter came to understand the person of Christ. In this book, Huntsperger portrays Peter as saying the following about his relationship with Christ (italics added):

> Whereas John [the Baptist] was most concerned with how his followers related to his message, Jesus was most concerned with how we related to him. But please don't misunderstand me here. I am not suggesting he wanted us to trot along at his side, hanging on his every word, with expressions of reverent awe and adoration on our faces. Far from it! It was clear from our first day together that what he valued most of all was our friendship. He obviously deeply enjoyed each of us. He really liked us.
>
> *We just knew this man loved us and valued our friendship as no one else had ever done before.* . . . Certainly his friendship produced profound changes in each of our lives. But they were not changes we attempted to paste on in order to be "good disciples of the great Teacher." *They were changes that gradually infiltrated our lives the more we relaxed in his unconditional love and acceptance.*[2]

I believe Huntsperger has captured the impact of Jesus' relational love in Peter's life. Peter later conveyed this same truth in his own words in 1 Peter 2:9–10 as he seeks to convey who we are in Christ. What point is Peter trying to drive home in these verses?

_____

_____

_____

FOR DEEPER REFLECTION

When you think of the human Jesus that walked on this earth, what mental image do you hold of Him? Try to describe below how you mentally picture Jesus.

The Scriptures tell us that Jesus "became flesh and made his dwelling among us" (John 1:14). At His core, He was God, but in the flesh we are told He had "no beauty or majesty to attract us to him, nothing in His appearance that we should desire him" (Isaiah 53:2b). Why do you think Jesus took on this type of appearance? What lesson are we to learn from this?

Entering Our World DAY 1

The God of the universe could have easily rented the Goodyear blimp and floated it around the globe flashing in neon lights: "I love you! Repent and believe!" Instead He chose to "become flesh" and dwell among us. The Greek word translated "dwell" literally means to "pitch up His tent in our midst." God made His home among us.

Jesus' ministry strategy reflects this same principle. He didn't rent large synagogues, put on a special program, and invite people to come hear Him preach. His whole strategy of impact was rooted in entering into people's real-world lives. He was constantly going where the people were, meeting their needs, and investing in them. His strategy was relational through and through. Jesus clearly understood that it is only to the degree in which we enter into people's lives is the degree to which we can expect them to enter into ours.

Jesus took on flesh to become like us so that He could identify with us in every way. And, ultimately, He came not to just initiate the relationship, but to continue that relationship by dying as the sacrificial Lamb of God who would take away the sins of the world. And through His Spirit in us, that relationship can continue ever deeper and deeper.

Jesus went to great lengths to identify with us. Matthew seemingly seeks to capture this in his gospel by illustrating how Jesus' life was orchestrated to identify with the nation of Israel. His flight into Egypt as a child with Mary and Joseph echoed Israel's "flight" to Egypt as a place of safety to escape the famine (Matthew 2:13–15). The slaughter of the innocent babies at Jesus' birth mirrored the same experience in the life of Moses (Exodus 4:19; Matthew 2:16–18). The forty days Jesus spent in the wilderness paralleled the forty years Israel spent in the wilderness. Matthew seeks to clearly show Jesus' relational identity with Israel.

Why do you think Matthew worked so hard to show Jesus' relational identity with the common person in Israel?

_____

_____

_____

Matthew's fellow Israelites, who tended to think they were better than the tax collectors and sinners, would have despised Matthew as a tax collector. No doubt Matthew was profoundly affected by Jesus' respect for him as a person.

In his genealogy, Matthew includes some men and women who were less than reputable in their days (Matthew 1:1–17). Matthew resonated deeply with how Jesus identified with the common sinner.

Where else do you see Jesus going to great extremes to identify with the needy people of His day?

_____

_____

_____

What impact did this have on people? Give an example.

_____

_____

_____

Do you agree that all life change comes through relationships? Why or why not?

_____

_____

_____

FOR DEEPER REFLECTION

The apostle Paul said, "Follow my example, as I follow the example of Christ" (1 Corinthians 11:1). In 1 Thessalonians 2:5–12, he describes his relational approach. Jot down how Paul described these relationships. What application might this have for you?

How does Paul's approach mirror what Jesus modeled? Be specific.

Taking Time DAY 2

As we discovered in a previous lesson, Jesus spent almost half of His ministry in relatively low profile, under the radar of John the Baptist's popularity. For the first eighteen months He ministered primarily in the Judean wilderness, in close proximity to his cousin, John.

During this time Jesus performed only two recorded miracles. The first was turning water into wine. The second miracle was the healing of the nobleman's son (John 4:47). Only after John was put into prison did Jesus begin to take up John's message Himself: "Repent for the kingdom of heaven is near" (Matthew 4:12–17).

If He wasn't in the limelight, Jesus was certainly busy for these eighteen months. John's popularity allowed Jesus the time and space to identify and invest in His disciples. Larry Huntsperger captures this well in *The Fisherman*, where he has Peter explaining this time alone with Jesus:

> I cannot overstate the importance of those early days we spent with the Master. All too soon the eyes of the entire nation would be turned on him, and our lives would take on a public intensity that would strip us of the casual privacy we shared during those first few weeks. Those weeks were enough for him to establish the ground rules that would shape our relationship with him forever.[3]

We do not have a lot of information about how Jesus spent the first few months of His ministry. But we have all that we need. What was Jesus doing during this time (John 3:22)? Explain why this is important.

_____

_____

_____

> The Christian faith is meant to be lived moment by moment. It isn't some broad, general outline —it's a long walk with a real Person. Details count: passing thoughts, small sacrifices, a few encouraging words, little acts of kindness, brief victories over nagging sins.
>
> —Joni Eareckson Tada

The word translated "spent time with" is the Greek word *diatribo*, which literally means "to get under the skin of" or "to rub off on." What image do these phrases give you of Jesus' time with His disciples? Why was it important for the disciples to get to know who Jesus really was?

_____

_____

_____

If change comes through relationships and all relationships take time, why do we need more and better relational disciple makers as our churches and ministries grow? What can happen in our churches and ministries (or our families, for that matter) if we try to bring about change only through activities or events?

_____

_____

_____

Ministry Jesus-style is about intentional loving relationships. What do you find most encouraging about this?

_____

_____

_____

What do you find most challenging about this truth?

_____

_____

_____

FOR DEEPER REFLECTION

What aspects of relationships can only happen with increased time together?

What does 1 John 3:16–18 tell us about relationships Jesus-style?

Loving People DAY 3

Bruce Marchiano, who brilliantly portrayed Jesus in *The Gospel According to Matthew* (DVD), was asked at one of our training events how he prepared, as an actor, to capture the personality of Jesus. He answered immediately: "As a young Christ follower, I knew I had to capture one major truth about Jesus. I had to be the most loving person I could imagine in order to convey Jesus well. But that love had to be both a tough and tender love."[4]

I believe Bruce understood the heart of Jesus well. To walk as Jesus walked, in intentional relationships, demands that our interactions with others be saturated with God's love. Anything less than this misses the whole point of walking as Jesus walked.

Today we are going to take a fresh look at 1 Corinthians 13, the "love chapter." This passage describes godly love. And because Jesus was God, it describes the walk of Jesus, the example we are to follow. Read the passage. Then spend a few moments reflecting on how Jesus must have related to His disciples.

Write down each word in 1 Corinthians 13:4–7 that describes what love is or isn't and then describe what this might have looked like in Jesus' relationships with His disciples. If possible, illustrate each observation with an event from the life of Jesus.

> If we truly love people, we will desire for them far more than it is within our power to give them, and this will lead us to prayer: Intercession is a way of loving others.
>
> —**Richard J. Foster**

    Love is   Jesus did these things

_____

_____

_____

_____

_____

_____

_____

_____

_____

Love is not	Jesus did these things

When people closest to you think of their relationship with you, which words from 1 Corinthians 13 would they most likely use to describe your relationship?

_____

_____

_____

Which words from 1 Corinthians 13 would you least likely use to describe yourself?

_____

_____

_____

John 1:14 describes Jesus as one who came full of "grace and truth." Read Luke 4:16–29 and write down how you see Jesus embodying these descriptions.

_____

_____

_____

Which is easier for you—demonstrating grace or truth? What happens when you have one without the other?

_____

_____

_____

FOR DEEPER REFLECTION

Look up 1 Corinthians 13:4–8 and write it below. Commit these verses to memory.

Why are both grace and truth needed in healthy relationships? Which do you most need from a friend right now? Why?

DAY 4 Friend of Sinners

Jesus' relationships with His disciples were never static. They continued to grow and deepen over time. The gospel of John presents this progression in Jesus' relationships clearly. In John 1:35–39, the disciples are presented as seekers curious about Jesus. Jesus' first words to these disciples are, "What do you want?" He invites them to "come and see," and He spends the day with them.

Soon Jesus invites the disciples to a more intimate level of fellowship. He invites them to "Follow Me." The Greek word used literally means "to walk alongside" or "walk closely in one's steps." The disciples accept Jesus' offer and they begin to grow in their relationships as Christ "followers."

By John 6, the disciples are "co-servants" with Jesus, as they help Him feed the five thousand. Their relationship had developed to the point that they were actively engaged in helping Jesus meet the needs of others. In John 13 Jesus wraps a towel around His waist and leaves them an example of what true servanthood should look like by washing their feet (John 13:15).

The relationship is at its deepest level by the time you get to John 15. Here Jesus calls His disciples "friends." By now He had made known to them everything He had learned from His Father. They have progressed from seekers to followers to co-servants to friends. Jesus was intentional about these relationships. His goal was to make His disciples His friends. In the next unit we will look at how Jesus deepened these friendships with His disciples.

However, the Scriptures record that Jesus was not only a "friend" to His disciples (John 15:15), but He was also a "friend of sinners." How is this phrase used in Matthew 11:18–19?

_____

_____

_____

In Matthew 9:10–13 Jesus is once again associated with "tax collectors and 'sinners.'" Why does Jesus say in this setting, "Go and learn what this means: 'I desire mercy, not sacrifice'"? What was Jesus modeling for us?

_____

_____

_____

In Luke 14:34–35, Jesus warns His listeners, "Salt is good, but if it loses its saltiness, how can it be made salty again? It is fit neither for the soil nor for the manure pile; it is thrown out." In the next verses (15:1–2) Jesus models an answer to this rhetorical question. Look closely at the situation. How does Jesus respond relationally to "sinners"?

_____

_____

_____

Why do you think the tax collectors and sinners felt so safe with Jesus? What insight does John 3:16–17 give us?

_____

_____

_____

Describe Jesus' attitude toward "tax collectors and 'sinners'" as it is presented in Luke 15:1–2. What type of attitude must you display so that lost people are eager to spend time with you?

_____

_____

_____

Who are the lost friends that the Lord has placed in your life? Those of us who have been active in church for a long time often feel disconnected from the lost. Our problem is simply what Jesus described in John 4:35: we need to open our "eyes and look at the fields! They are ripe for harvest." Our research suggests that the average churchgoer has more than twenty relationships with non-Christians. The lost are there in your world of relationships, if we just open our eyes to see them. Take a moment to make a list of people you know need the Lord.

Never let a problem to be solved become more important than a person to be loved.

—Barbara Johnson

Family members (immediate family) who don't know the Lord

_____

_____

_____

Relatives (extended family) who don't know the Lord

_____

_____

_____

Neighbors who don't know the Lord

_____

_____

_____

Work associates who don't know the Lord

_____

_____

_____

Acquaintances (mail carrier, mechanic, doctor, etc.) who don't know the Lord

_____

_____

_____

Choose two people from the lists above you feel the Lord would have you prioritize. What can you do in the next few weeks to deepen these relationships?

_____

_____

_____

FOR DEEPER REFLECTION

Why is it important for us, like Jesus, to have friendships with the lost? How do such relationships encourage our relationship with the Father to keep growing? See Philemon 6.

Take some time to pray for those people you listed above.

DAY 5 Eternal CPR

Jesus intentionally became a "friend of sinners" to demonstrate the remarkable love of God for His creation. Jesus' mission was to seek and save those who were lost (Luke 19:10). We celebrate this mission, because we have benefited from it, lost sinners that we were. But the faithful Jews of Jesus' time were scandalized by Jesus' approach. Jesus knew that it was not the healthy but the sick who need a doctor (Matthew 9:12). But for first-century Jews, there were certain people who were simply off limits.

Early in His ministry, Jesus shocked His disciples when He told them "he had to go through Samaria" (John 4:4). No good Jew traveled through Samaria. In the Jewish mind, Samaritans were often viewed as half-breed Jews who intermarried with the Assyrians when the Northern Kingdom was conquered in 722 BC. As a result they were religious compromisers who held to a different place of worship. But Jesus wanted to model compassion for the people of Samaria, a compassion He expected His disciples to emulate. In particular, Jesus interacts with a Samaritan woman who seems to have been rejected in the region because she had been married five times. Through her influence, the whole town came out to see Jesus, to see if He could indeed be the Christ (John 4:29).

What Jesus models here is a heart of genuine love; or, as I like to call it, Eternal CPR.[5] Physical CPR is caring for the emergency needs of a heart gone bad. Eternal CPR is caring for the spiritual needs of a heart gone bad through cultivating (C), planting (P), and reaping (R).

Farmers intuitively understand the process of reaping a harvest. Any farmer knows that reaping a harvest is a lengthy process. The first step is breaking up the hardened ground to receive the seed. This is accomplished by cultivating the soil and this is often the hardest part (John 4:38). After cultivation comes planting; carefully placing the seed in the right way, at the right depth, and at the right time (John 4:37). When done properly, this process will lead to reaping a rich harvest. This is the joy of farming, seeing the harvest happen.

In the same way, being a friend of sinners like Jesus is a process that must be developed. Eternal CPR is that process. Cultivating is becoming a friend of sinners and often takes time and energy. Planting is placing the seeds of truth into that friendship at the right time, in the right way, and the right depth. Reaping is clearly and concisely presenting the good news of salvation to our friends. This process can be quick, but it is often slow. Either way, it is God who gives the increase.

Read Isaiah 28:23–29. What does this passage say about the cultivating process?

_____

_____

_____

What does this passage say about the planting process? How many different types of seeds are sown? What spiritual application might this have?

_____

_____

_____

What words of encouragement do you find in these verses for when we don't feel we are very good at Eternal CPR? (See Isaiah 28:23, 26, 29.)

_____

_____

_____

Can you see each of these three steps in the life of Christ? Give some examples.

_____

_____

_____

Choose three of the non-Christian friends you listed last time. What could you do this week to move that friendship forward to the next step of Eternal CPR?

_____

_____

_____

FOR DEEPER REFLECTION

Which step of the Eternal CPR process is most difficult for you? Why do you think that is?

Think through your own journey of coming to Christ. Who did the cultivating? Who planted? Who reaped in your life? First Corinthians 3:5–8 tells us that different people play different roles. Have you ever thanked these various people for the role they played in your coming to faith? Maybe a quick note of thanks would be appropriate and greatly appreciated.

WEEKS 1–8 SUMMARY

1. Jesus is our model for life and ministry and we are commanded to "walk as He walked."

2. In His humanity, Jesus was man as God intended mankind to be, showing us how to walk.

3. The first foundational priority we see in Jesus' humanity was total dependence on the Holy Spirit in everything He did.

4. The second priority we see is how Jesus "often slipped away to pray." He lived a life of prayerful guidance.

5. Third, out of reverent submission, Jesus learned obedience and calls us to that same lifestyle of obedience.

6. Fourth, Jesus trusted, studied, learned from, and submitted to the Scriptures. He used the Scriptures as He approached the demands of living a holy life. He was Word-centered.

7. Fifth, Jesus always exalted His Father as the source of everything.

8. Sixth, Jesus lived a life of intentional loving relationships, becoming a friend of sinners as well as a friend to His disciples. His strategy was relational.

INVESTING IN A FEW

See WalkingAsJesus.com for video resources specific to this week's study.

GETTING STARTED

I n the past section we looked at Jesus' relational strategy. We observed how Jesus was not only a "friend of sinners" but also a "friend" to His disciples. As we continue in this study on Walking as Jesus Walked, we now want to focus on some of the ways in which Jesus deepened those relationships with a few.

We also discussed in a previous section how Jesus voluntarily accepted the limitations of humanity when He chose to take on flesh and walk among us. For example, He was not omnipresent in His humanity. As a result, He had to set priorities when He woke up every morning—just as you and I do. Just like ours, Jesus' days were only twenty-four hours long!

But unlike many of us, Jesus was aware of the limitations of being human. We have hundreds of relationships and can feel frustrated that we can't develop them all. We feel pulled in so many directions and try to please everyone. Consequently, we develop few deep friendships.

Jesus knew better. About eighteen months into His ministry, He began to invest His time in just a few disciples. In Mark 1:16–20 (and Matthew 4:18–22) Jesus singles out four individuals and challenges them to a deeper level of involvement with Him. Perhaps He saw that these men were AFTER more.[1] Luke 5:1–11 tells us that each of them were:

> If the Son of God thought it necessary to focus his life on a small group of men, we are fooling ourselves to think we can mass-produce disciples today. God's design for taking the gospel to the world is a slow, intentional, simple process that involves every one of His people sacrificing every facet of their lives to multiply the life of Christ in others.
>
> —David Platt

WALKING AS JESUS WALKED

Available (Luke 5:1–3)

Faithful (Luke 5:4–5)

Teachable (Luke 5:6–8)

Enthused (Luke 5:9–10)

Responsive (Luke 5:11)

Jesus had already developed a relationship with each of these disciples. This is not His first contact with them. However, it is the first time He challenges them to join His mission of multiplication. He tells them He will make them fishers of men. From this point on Jesus changes the focus of His ministry. In the first eighteen months of His ministry, For the rest of His ministry, He prioritizes His time with a few men.

In his book *The Master Plan of Evangelism*, Robert Coleman calls this the "genius of Christ's ministry." His mission was not so much to reach the whole world as to make disciples who would reach the whole world. *This is a subtle but life-changing distinction*.

We would do well to follow Jesus' example and invest in the few people God has placed in our lives who are AFTER more!

Our greatest impact in life will be made not among the masses but in the few people we pour our life into. This makes walking as Jesus walked very practical. Who are the few you are prioritizing? This question can liberate you from the tyranny of trying to please everyone.

Look closely at Mark 1:16–20. Who are the four that Jesus first called into a closer relationship with Him?

_____

_____

_____

Think about your relationships. Who are two or three people you think the Lord is leading you to go deeper with?

_____

_____

_____

What do you think these people might need? Maybe some have broken relationships or broken lives that need repairing. Maybe they are relationally healthy and just need to be more prepared to join in Jesus' mission of multiplication. Write your reflections below.

Name	Greatest Need	Why?

FOR DEEPER REFLECTION

List some of the practical relational limitations Jesus placed on Himself in His humanity. How does this list encourage you that you can be a friend like Jesus?

What keeps you from deepening your relationships with just a few people? Be specific.

DAY 1 Going Deeper

For the next few days, we are going to focus our attention on the gospel of Mark where we will explore how Jesus developed His relationship with four disciples in whom He invested the greatest amount of time and energy. We want to discover how we can go deeper with the few people the Lord has placed around us. We want to know what it means to walk as Jesus walked in intentional relationships.

Immediately after Jesus invites these four into deeper relationship, saying, "Follow me, and I will make you fishers of men," He takes them to Capernaum. What does He do with them there (Mark 1:21–22)?

_____

_____

_____

After this experience in the synagogue, Jesus heads somewhere else (Mark 1:29–30). Where does He go? Why?

_____

_____

_____

Twice Jesus spends time in Peter's home (Mark 1:29; 14:3) and once in Matthew's home (Matthew 9:10). Jesus left His heavenly home to enter into our earthly home. He realized the practical implications of a deeper relationship.

If we hope to develop a deeper relationship with a person, why is it important to spend time in their world (home)? What can you learn in someone's home that you can't learn elsewhere?

_____

_____

_____

What does this encounter with Jesus in Peter's home (Mark 1:29) tell us about Peter's needs? Why is it important that we understand the needs and pressures our "few" are facing?

_____

_____

_____

Why did Jesus say that He must go elsewhere when the crowds were looking for Him (Mark 1:36–38)? What lesson was Jesus modeling for His few disciples? How does this apply to your few?

_____

_____

_____

FOR DEEPER REFLECTION

If we never enter into the real world of our disciples (our few), what can be the consequences?

If we never let our disciples enter into our real world, what can be the consequences?

DAY 2 Ministering Together

Several times during His ministry, Jesus led His disciples on short-term mission trips. These were trips where Jesus specifically involved His disciples in experiences that demanded more time with Him and involved them in ministry alongside of Him. We saw the first of these trips in John 4 when they had to go through Samaria. This trip took place about a year into Jesus' ministry and lasted approximately one to two weeks. This radical cross-cultural experience was just the beginning for Jesus' disciples!

The gospel of Mark records the second of Jesus' short-term mission trips (Mark 1:39). It appears that Jesus went out on these trips about every six months (John 4:4, Mark 1:39, Luke 8:1–3, Matthew 9:35–10:1, and Luke 10:1–17). Each trip is more extensive than the previous and increasingly demands more from the disciples. Jesus is gradually developing His disciples by in-the-field training. This had been His goal all along.

The trip throughout Galilee referenced in Mark 1:39 may have lasted up to two months. Where did Jesus go and what did He do during that time? What do you think His disciples learned from Him?

_____

_____

_____

Ministering together outside of our daily routines is a great learning experience. An extended mission or ministry trip over several days gives us dozens of hours together. What might be the benefit of a mission trip that lasted more than just a few days—maybe months? What did Jesus and His disciples gain from this type of experience that they couldn't have experienced in daily living?

_____

_____

_____

What are some practical ways in which you could spend some extended time with your "few"?

_____

_____

_____

FOR DEEPER REFLECTION

Read through John 4 and list all the things that Jesus' disciples might have learned from Him.

What do you think the disciples learned as they traveled throughout Galilee and heard Jesus preach in the synagogues and cast out demons (Mark 1:39)? Be practical and specific in your observations.

DAY 3 Keeping the Healthy . . . Healthy

By this point in His ministry, Jesus had come to appreciate the value of solitude. It was customary for Him, after a busy period of ministry, to get away alone to a deserted place. Jesus wanted His disciples to learn to make this a priority, too. He knew that if He failed to keep His best disciples healthy, they would be unable to keep others healthy. So Jesus modeled for them the value of restorative solitude.

Read Mark 6:30–32. In your own words, describe what is happening here.

_____

_____

_____

> **No one can sum up all God is able to accomplish through one solitary life, wholly yielded, adjusted, and obedient to Him.**
>
> **—D. L. Moody**

When people in our ministry are healthy, we often work them to death. We push them until they burn out and then abandon them. Jesus knew better. He recognized that His role was to invest in His key workers teaching the value of solitude, keeping them healthy, and equipping them so they in turn could help others become healthy. Such a simple principle, but so easily forgotten!

What happens in our family, church, business, or ministry if we fail to invest in the health of our "few"?

_____

_____

_____

What are the main indicators for you that you are becoming unhealthy and may be in need of solitude?

_____

_____

_____

FOR DEEPER REFLECTION

What happens when you get unhealthy in your daily walk? What are the consequences? Who suffers?

What do you think Jesus might have experienced in the wilderness that He wanted His disciples to experience themselves?

DAY 4 Caring Enough to Confront

Jesus spent quite a bit of His time confronting the insincere religiosity He perceived in the Pharisees and teachers of the Law. On one occasion, He quoted the prophet Isaiah (see Isaiah 29:13) and called these religious leaders hypocrites who honor God with their lips but keep their hearts far from Him. Moreover, He said, these religious leaders had abandoned the commands of God and were holding dear traditions created by men. Not exactly a seeker-friendly message!

> The decision to grow always involves a choice between risk and comfort. This means that to be a follower of Jesus you must renounce comfort as the ultimate value of your life.
>
> —John Ortberg

In a parallel passage in Matthew 15:12, the disciples pull Jesus aside and try to straighten Him out. "Do you know that the Pharisees were offended when they heard this?" they asked. What an understatement! How I would love to have been a fly on the wall when this exchange happened. What was Jesus' expression like? How did He handle this attempted rebuke? What were the disciples feeling that caused them to confront Jesus?

Jesus then takes them aside and enters a house. This statement in Mark 7:17 implies that Jesus was alone with the disciples, since the homes were small and the crowd was now outside. Look at Mark 7:18. What does Jesus say to them?

_____

_____

_____

The word "dull" that Jesus uses literally means "so slow to learn" or "unintelligent." This was not a gentle rebuke. It was forceful. Jesus cares enough about His disciples to confront them!

Give an example from your life when someone has cared enough to confront you.

_____

_____

_____

How did you respond? Read Proverbs 9:8–9. Who appreciates confrontation? What are the benefits?

_____

_____

_____

If you don't care enough to confront your few, who will? Caring enough to confront has become a lost art, one that is integral to true disciple making. Jesus modeled this with His disciples, and He expects us to do it with our few. Confrontation must take place in deep, safe relationships, and it must be done correctly. But ultimately it is a sign of respect and genuine concern.

On a scale of 1 to 10, how good are you at confronting? Explain your answer below.

| 1 | 2 | 3 | 4 | 5 | 6 | 7 | 8 | 9 | 10 |

Avoid at all costs   Confront with love and wisdom

_____

_____

_____

What are some lessons you have learned from experience, either good or bad, about confronting someone with love and wisdom?

_____

_____

_____

FOR DEEPER REFLECTION

What are the major skills necessary to successfully confront someone who needs to be corrected?

Often we deal with confrontation as it was dealt with in our family as we were growing up. How was confrontation handled in your family? What were some positives and negatives about this?

DAY 5 Go and Die

This week, we have discussed several difficult lessons Jesus wanted His disciples, and us, to learn about living in relationship. Today we will explore what is by far the most challenging lesson of all.

After a twenty-mile trip north of His ministry headquarters in Capernaum, Jesus took His disciples into Caesarea Philippi. Here, Jesus asked Peter, "Who do people say I am?" After listening to their responses, He then follows up this question: "But what about you? Who do you say that I am?"

Peter then gives the confession of faith that he has become known for, "You are the Christ" (Mark 8:27–29).

This is a high point for Peter. He finally understands who Jesus is!

But now, Jesus begins to take on a more serious tone with His disciples. He begins to explain that "the Son of Man must suffer many things and be rejected . . . killed . . . and . . .rise again" (Mark 8:31).

Peter can't stand it. He takes Jesus aside and tries to rebuke Him. But Jesus rebukes Peter instead. "Get behind me, Satan!" He says. "You do not have in mind the things of God, but the things of men" (Mark 8:33).

What a statement! It appears that Satan, working through Peter's words, was tempting Jesus to avoid death on the cross. Consequently, Jesus rebuked Peter (and Satan) for trying to thwart God's plan. For these last nine months of His life, Jesus sets His heart toward Jerusalem and ultimately the cross. Twice more He will remind His disciples that He must go to Jerusalem to suffer, die, and then rise again.

But His message to His disciples gets even more difficult.

Jesus tells those closest to Him that anyone who wants to be His disciple must also "deny himself and take up his cross and follow me. For whoever wants to save his life will lose it, but whoever loses his life for me will find it" (Matthew 16:24–25).

The Christian life, the life of following Jesus, is a journey to the cross.

It's a journey that requires saying no to self and yes to God. What a message! A promise of joy, reward, and fullness, indeed; but also a promise of suffering, servanthood, and sacrifice.

Jesus' relational challenge had progressed from "Come and see" (John 1:39), to "Follow me" (John 1:43), to "Follow me and I will make you fishers of men" (Matthew 4:19). Now His ultimate challenge was to "go and bear fruit" (John 15:16), or as some have said, "go and die." It is the lifelong challenge of dying to self and allowing His Holy Spirit to live in and through us!

Investing in our few means helping them see that the Christian life is ultimately a life of denying ourselves and taking up our crosses daily to follow Jesus. How do you feel about this challenge?

> Until you have given up your self to Him you will not have a real self . . .
>
> —C. S. Lewis

_____

_____

_____

How do you live out this message of Jesus practically?

_____

_____

_____

How can we cultivate this message in our few?

_____

_____

_____

FOR DEEPER REFLECTION

Read the parable of the sower and the seed (Luke 8:4–15) aloud. What keeps people from denying themselves and following Jesus?

What happens when we fail to prepare our disciples for the ultimate call of the Christian life . . . to suffer, serve, and sacrifice . . . like Christ did?

WEEKS 1–9 SUMMARY

1. Jesus is our model for life and ministry and we are commanded to "walk as He walked."

2. In His humanity, Jesus was man as God intended man to be, showing us how to walk.

3. The first foundational priority we see in Jesus' humanity was total dependence on the Holy Spirit in everything He did.

4. The second priority we see is how Jesus "often slipped away to pray." He lived a life of prayerful guidance.

5. Third, out of reverent submission, Jesus learned obedience and calls us to that same lifestyle of obedience.

6. Fourth, Jesus trusted, studied, learned from, and submitted to the Scriptures. He used the Scriptures as He approached the demands of living a holy life. He was Word-centered.

7. Fifth, Jesus always exalted His Father as the source of everything.

8. Sixth, Jesus lived a life of intentional loving relationships, becoming a friend of sinners as well as a friend to His disciples. His strategy was relational.

9. Jesus poured His life into a few, creating a movement of multiplying disciples.

JESUS AND MULTIPLICATION

See WalkingAsJesus.com for video resources specific to this week's study.

GETTING STARTED

As I have studied and taught the life of Christ over the years, I have developed two deep convictions about Jesus' life and ministry.

The first is that Jesus' life and ministry was intended to create a movement of multiplication. The personal calling of Jesus, the Father's will for Him, was to provide atonement for the sins of all mankind (Matthew 26:39; Isaiah 53:10). This was His personal calling, which He fulfilled completely.

But His ministry calling was different. His "work" (John 17:4) was to create a movement of multiplying disciples . . . that is, disciples who could make disciples. The fully human Jesus poured His life into a few chosen disciples and equipped them to do the same. The evidence of the disciples' fruitfulness is overwhelming. Within two years they "filled Jerusalem" (Acts 5:28). In just over four years they were multiplying churches (Acts 9:31). Within nineteen years, they "turned the world upside down" (Acts 17:6 NKJV). Within thirty years, Colossians tells us, "all over the world this gospel is bearing fruit and growing" (Colossians 1:6).

My second conviction about the life and ministry of Jesus is that Jesus commanded us to "do what I have been doing" (John 14:12) and "do as I have done for you" (John 13:15). His apostle John reminds us that "whoever claims to live in him must walk as Jesus did" (1 John 2:6). Jesus was clear that to the degree to which we walk as He walked, we can expect to do what He did.

As a matter of fact, Jesus even promises that we will do even greater things than He did (John 14:12).

How can this be? To begin with, we have more time. While Jesus had less than four years to make disciples, we, by God's grace, can have forty years or more to make disciples. Take the apostle Paul, for example. Jesus' brief ministry ended with eleven leaders and 120 timid disciples in the upstairs room in Jerusalem (Acts 1:13). Paul, in about sixteen years of ministry, planted multiple churches in multiple countries and equipped more than forty leaders to follow in his footsteps. Jesus' promise in John 14:12 that His followers "will do even greater things than these," was fulfilled in Paul's life; because Paul walked as Jesus walked and encouraged his followers to "follow my example, as I follow the example of Christ" (1 Corinthians 11:1).

Reread John 14:10–15. According to Jesus, how did He accomplish the things He accomplished?

_____

_____

_____

Like Jesus, we are called to allow God to work through us to bear fruit. This is the reason we've been chosen (John 15:16).

The power of multiplication

From beginning to end, Scripture is clear that God's strategy for world impact is multiplication. Early in Genesis, God established this principle when He said, "It is good. . . . God blessed them. . . . be fruitful and multiply" (Genesis 1:12, 28 NKJV). Goodness always accompanies God's blessing, blessing always leads to fruitfulness, and fruitfulness always results in multiplication.

Have you ever considered the power of multiplication? One day while I was first considering this concept, I asked my twelve-year-old daughter if she would rather have $1 a day doubled for 30 days or $1,000,000 a day for 30 days. Julie was very much into math and immediately began to try to calculate the problem in her head. $1 a day doubled equals $1 plus $1 equals $2 (day 1). Two dollars plus $2 equals $4 (day 2). Four dollars plus $4 equals $8 (day 3). Eight dollars plus $8 equals $16 (day 4). And so on. After a couple of minutes of mental math, she threw up her arms and said, "Oh Dad, just give me the $30,000,000. I'll be happy with that!"

This is an exercise in compound interest. One dollar a day doubled for 30 days equals over $2.1 billion. That's 714 times the principle of addition. Behold the power of multiplication.

Let me give you another example, more to the point. How long would it take to win the world for Christ if just one person could lead 1,000 people to Him every day? If you do the math, it would take over 17,500 years, and that is if no one else was born in that span of time.

By contrast, how long would it take you to win the world to Christ if you follow Jesus' pattern of multiplication? What would happen if you win one person to Christ every six months and disciple him or her to lead someone else to Christ and then repeat the process with others?

The answer is staggering. The disciple-making Christ followers would win the world to Christ in seventeen years through the power of multiplication. Of course this illustration assumes no failure and no sin (impossible in our world system). Nevertheless, it is an illustration of the power of Jesus' method.

Read Matthew 25:14–30. How do you see the principle of multiplication at work in this passage?

_____

_____

_____

How do you see the principle of multiplication in Matthew 13:1–9? Explain.

_____

_____

_____

FOR DEEPER REFLECTION

How might your priorities change if you focused on multiplication?

Describe a time when you have experienced the principle of multiplication at work in life.

DAY 1 Fruit and Multiplication

A number of years ago during a particularly busy time in our ministry, we led a conference for hundreds of Christian leaders. Afterward, our leadership team stayed a few extra days to debrief. It was a sweet reprieve when we had felt surrounded by chaos. One evening we kicked back and reminisced about life, our families, and the joy of our ministry partnership. We had been through a lot together, and this calm in the thick of the storms of our busy lives gave us a chance to truly enjoy one another's friendship.

I've often thought that this is what Jesus' time with His disciples in the upper room must have been like. Amidst the battles of life, Jesus took a moment to enjoy His disciples' friendship, a much needed calm before the pending storm.

Soon after this time, Jesus and His friends left the upper room and headed down to the garden of Gethsemane. On this last night together before His death on the cross, Jesus speaks some of His final words to His disciples. I'm sure He selected them carefully. The setting, it seems, is a vineyard. Here in His final hours, Jesus talks to His disciples about bearing fruit.

Read John 15:1–17. What are the four levels of fruit-bearing Jesus mentions?

_____

_____

_____

Of which level does Jesus say "This is to my Father's glory"?

_____

_____

_____

Who is the vine? Who is the gardener? What are we in this illustration?

_____

_____

_____

What is the fruit? (See also Galatians 5:22–23, Romans 1:13, and Philippians 1:11.)

_____

_____

_____

FOR DEEPER REFLECTION

What is our role in producing fruit? (See John 12:24.)

Can you make anything grow? What is our role in bringing about growth? (See 1 Corinthians 3:5–8.)

DAY 2 From No Fruit to Some Fruit

We have discovered four levels of fruit-bearing in John 15 . . . no fruit, fruit, more fruit, and much fruit. We also discovered that Jesus' passion and plan for His followers (and that means us) is that we "bear much fruit, showing yourselves to be my disciples" (John 15:8). What a calling!

If we are to do this, it is important that we look at the process Jesus describes here for producing "much fruit." Just as there are barriers that keep companies and churches from growing to the next level, so there are barriers that keep us from being fruitful. If we are aware of those barriers, we will know better what we can do to aid the Gardener in bearing more fruit.

As you initially think about what keeps you from producing fruit, what would you identify as some of those barriers?

_____

_____

_____

The worst condition we can be in is producing "no fruit." In the NIV translation, verse 2 tells us that the gardener "cuts off every branch in me that bears no fruit." The Greek word translated here as "cuts off" can be rendered another way that seems to fit this context better. The Greek word literally means "to lift up" or "to move to a different location." It is the same word used in Mark 2:11, when Jesus tells the paralytic, "take up your mat and go home." Lift it up and go someplace else. Even in a well-tended vineyard, vines sometimes fall off the carefully made fence down into the dirt and mud and out of the sunlight. If they stay there long enough, they wither and become like a branch that is thrown away and burned (John 15:6).

When a good gardener sees such a branch, he will lift it up, carefully clean it off, and place it back in the sunlight so that it will eventually bear fruit.

Let's take this insight back to our passage. Jesus is talking about "every branch in me." Throughout the New Testament, the phrase "in me" (or "in Christ") describes a Christian. In other words, Jesus is talking in this passage about those Christians who, for whatever reason, get down in the dirt of sin and out of the sunlight (Son light).

This may surprise you. Can a person be in Christ and not bear fruit? Has there ever been a period in your Christian life when you have been out of the Son's light and stuck in sin? Jesus is implying that it is possible to be a Christian but not bear fruit—at least for a season. Reflect for a moment about a season in your life when this was true. Describe it below.

_____

_____

_____

Fruit in the Scriptures is measured as Christian character (Galatians 5:22–23), conduct (Philippians 1:11), and conversions (Romans 1:13). Fruit grows as we walk in the Spirit of God and He works through us. Every person in Christ has the Spirit living within him or her. So if we have never seen any fruit in our lives, we need to examine ourselves to see if we do indeed have Christ's Spirit within us (2 Corinthians 13:5). No fruit—ever—may mean we have no relationship with Christ. But even those of us in Christ can grieve and quench the Spirit by allowing unconfessed sin to remain in our life. We will not bear fruit in this condition. Getting out of the mud and back into the Son light is the only way to begin bearing fruit. Write 1 John 1:5–9 below and ask the Lord to show you clearly if there is any unconfessed sin reigning in your life.

_____

_____

_____

We cannot produce fruit through our own abilities. We are just branches. Our job is to abide in Him and remain in the Son's light, allowing the Spirit of God to flow through us to produce the fruit.

FOR DEEPER REFLECTION

How does this illustration of the vine and branches make more sense if we translate the Greek word to mean "lift up" rather than "cut off" (in John 15:2)? What could be some of the difficulties of translating this word as "lift up"?

Read Galatians 5:22–23, Philippians 1:11, and Romans 1:13. Do you agree that these verses summarize what it means to bear fruit—character, conduct, and converts?

We want to avoid suffering, death, sin, ashes. But we live in a world crushed and broken and torn, a world God Himself visited to redeem. We receive His poured-out life, and, being allowed the high privilege of suffering with Him, may then pour ourselves out for others.

–Elisabeth Elliot

DAY 3 From Some Fruit to More Fruit

Last time we discovered what keeps us from bearing spiritual fruit. Today, as Jesus continues to lead His disciples through the vine and branches illustration, He now explains how we can move from producing some fruit to producing more fruit. Read John 15:2 and write down how Jesus says this process happens. You may not like His answer.

_____

_____

_____

A number of years ago, I toured the largest home in America, the Biltmore Estate in Asheville, North Carolina. The home on this 8,000-acre estate is more than 125,000 square feet and has 250 rooms. Impressive! But that's not what caught my attention. Toward the back of the property is a beautiful vineyard. I met one of the gardeners there and took the opportunity to discuss with him his practice of pruning. To my surprise, he told me that you could acquire a doctorate in pruning alone. I had no idea there was enough to know about pruning that you could earn a doctorate in the subject! Needless to say, I learned a lot from our conversation.

The gardener explained to me that a master gardener carefully studies every plant, and he rarely prunes two plants in exactly the same way. Each plant is unique. Careful pruning can add years to the fruitfulness of a plant. Likewise, failure to prune will result in a snarled branch that expends all its energy just keeping the branch alive. This means little sap is used in producing actual fruit. All the sap goes to maintaining the existing branches.

But even productive branches must be pruned. Many branches can produce multiple clusters of fruit, so a master gardener studies each branch carefully and prunes the ten or twelve clusters down to only two or three. This way the branch will produce richer and more desirable fruit. If what keeps us from producing any fruit is sin, the natural barrier to producing *more fruit* is having too many clusters of fruit—too much stuff.

I see many Christians consumed with too much good stuff in their lives. None of it is sin. But all this good stuff keeps them from focusing on the best stuff (see Philippians 1:10).

> All of God's people are ordinary people who have been made extraordinary by the purpose He has given them.
>
> —Oswald Chambers

If we don't prune back the good stuff, the Lord will do it. He wants us to produce *much fruit*. Doing few things but doing them well is often much better than doing many things with mediocrity.

Much to my delight, the gardener also shared with me that he is a Christian. He told me that although pruning is healthy, "we should never pray for pruning, but we should expect it." Pruning is painful and it always comes before the harvest.

We then began to discuss Hebrews 12:4–11. Read this passage and write down if this sounds like pruning to you.

_____

_____

_____

I asked the gardener the difference between discipline (Hebrews 12:7) and pruning (John 15:2). Both come from the Lord. Both are for our good. Both can be painful. But I wanted to know how to tell the difference. When you are going through a difficult time, how do you discern whether you are experiencing discipline or pruning? What do you think?

_____

_____

_____

> Start by doing what's necessary; then do what's possible; and suddenly you are doing the impossible.
>
> —Francis of Assisi

I was amazed at the gardener's answer. This Christian brother simply said, "Ask Him! The Lord loves you and will tell you! If it's discipline, He will show you the road to returning to Him. If it's pruning, He will give you the grace to endure."

God's agenda for each of us is to move us from producing some fruit to producing more fruit. Take a moment and thank God for how He is doing that in your life right now.

_____

_____

_____

FOR DEEPER REFLECTION

What needs to be pruned in your life so you can produce more fruit?

Why can less often be more? Give an example from your life when pruning back literally produced more.

From More Fruit to Much Fruit DAY 4

We have seen how to move from producing no fruit to producing some fruit. Today we will see that Jesus desires for each of us to produce much fruit. He mentions this in John 15:5 and 15:8. What do these verses have in common? What is the different emphasis of each?

_____

_____

_____

Eleven times in John 15:1–10 Jesus uses the word "remain." "Remain in Me," Jesus says, "and I will remain in you" (15:4). On the other hand, He also describes what happens if we fail to remain in Him. List all the verses in John 15 where Jesus uses the word "remain."

_____

_____

_____

The Greek word translated "remain" in this passage is rich in meaning. It is the word *meno*. It can also be translated as "abide," "dwell," "continue," and "endure." A form of the word appears in John 14:2 where Jesus says, "In my Father's house are many *rooms* (dwelling places)." It also appears in John 14:23, where Jesus says, "If anyone loves me . . . My Father will love him, and we will come to him and *make our home* with him." In other words, Jesus is commanding His disciples to "continue to make Me your permanent dwelling place." The only way we can move from producing more fruit to producing much fruit is by remaining in Christ.

One common barrier that often keeps us from moving from more fruit to much fruit is satisfaction. We can be satisfied with the more fruit, content with the good things the Lord is doing in our lives, and forget that He wants to get us to *much fruit*. To produce much fruit, we have to stop being content with producing more fruit. We have to seek Christ desperately, abide in Him, and allow Him to show us how to produce much fruit. Only He can do it.

I have seen it happen many times—a simple idea, a new thought, a perfectly timed God-connection can produce *much fruit*. Then all the praise and glory goes to Him. But this only happens when we abide in Christ, making Jesus our permanent dwelling place.

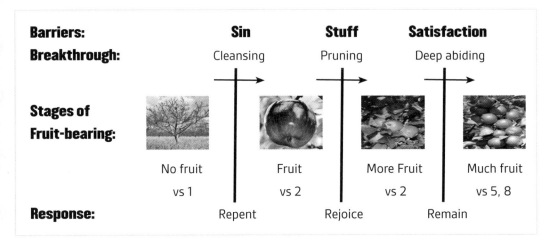

Barriers:	**Sin**	**Stuff**	**Satisfaction**
Breakthrough:	Cleansing	Pruning	Deep abiding

Stages of Fruit-bearing:	No fruit	Fruit	More Fruit	Much fruit
	vs 1	vs 2	vs 2	vs 5, 8
Response:	Repent	Rejoice	Remain	

Where are you in this process? What is your next step? What barrier do you need to overcome?

_____

_____

_____

FOR DEEPER REFLECTION

Read John 15:5. Notice that Jesus did not say, "Apart from me you cannot do much." He says we can do nothing. Do you believe this? Or do you sometimes feel that by yourself you can do quite a lot, and Jesus can help you do more if you need Him? How might this attitude hinder fruitfulness in your life? Can you give an example?

At which level of fruit-bearing do you feel you are living today? What do you think is the Lord's next step for you?

Fewer than 3 percent of Christians ever feel they arrive at the "much fruit" stage. Why do you think this is? What is God's stated desire for each of us (see John 15:8)?

Gaining by Giving DAY 5

This week we have explored Jesus' process of producing fruit in our lives. But our task is not complete. There is one more thing we must know before we can live the fully abundant life Jesus calls us to live. Jesus often said that we gain by giving, most famously that to gain your life you must lose it (Luke 9:24–25). Philemon 6 gets at this point in a different way. Write it below (use the NIV, if you have it).

_____

_____

_____

Paul tells us here that as we share our faith, we gain full understanding of every good thing we have in Christ Jesus. We gain it as we give it away.

Do you want to truly walk as Jesus walked? When you teach something, you begin to really understand it. Consider partnering in the faith—with Jesus, with Paul, and with thousands of other Christians around the globe—and share with others what you have learned in this study about walking as Jesus walked.

Who do you know that could benefit from working through this material with you? Who has the Lord placed in your life that you could lead through this study about walking as Jesus walked? Jot their names down here.

_____

_____

_____

Can you imagine what could happen if you took your friend through this study? Maybe the Lord could use you to create a movement of multiplying disciples who are walking as Jesus walked. Of course, you can't do this in your own strength. Jesus knew that! But you can do it if you walk as He walked, leaning on the following resources:

Holy Spirit Dependence

Prayerful guidance

Obedient living

Word-centered

Exalting the Father

Relational focus

Here's my challenge: Ask the few people you listed above if they'd like to learn more about Jesus and what it means to walk as He walked. Trust the **Holy Spirit** for leading and wisdom. **Pray** regularly for those He sends to you. Learn **obedience** by stepping out in faith. Study the **Word** and discuss it with your friends. **Exalt the Father** in all that happens. Love and care **relationally** for those friends by imparting your life to them. Then *you will be walking as Jesus walked*! This is not complicated. It just takes obedience and faith. "Trust and obey, for there is no other way," the hymn says.

May Jesus richly bless you and lead you into much fruit as you seek to "walk as He walked"!

FOR DEEPER REFLECTION

Can you think of a time in your life when you really began to understand something only after you taught it to someone else? Reflect on that experience.

What concerns do you have about leading others through this study? How could living out the **H***oly* **S***pirit* **POWER** *help you overcome these fears?*

WEEKS 1-10 SUMMARY

In review, we have concluded the following about "walking as Jesus walked":

1. Jesus is our model for life and ministry and we are commanded to "walk as He walked."

2. In His humanity, Jesus was man as God intended mankind to be, showing us how to walk.

3. The first foundational priority we see in Jesus' humanity was total dependence on the Holy Spirit in everything He did.

4. The second priority we see is how Jesus "often slipped away to pray." He lived a life of prayerful guidance.

5. Third, out of reverent submission, Jesus learned obedience and calls us to that same lifestyle of obedience.

6. Fourth, Jesus trusted, studied, learned from, and submitted to the Scriptures. He used the Scriptures as He approached the demands of living a holy life. He was Word-centered.

7. Fifth, Jesus always exalted His Father as the source of everything.

8. Sixth, Jesus lived a life of intentional loving relationships, becoming a friend of sinners as well as a friend to His disciples. His strategy was relational.

9. Jesus poured His life into a few, creating a movement of multiplying disciples.

10. Jesus' goal is for each of us to "walk as He walked," bearing much fruit and so proving to be His disciples. We can do this by the power of the Holy Spirit, prayer, obedience, the Word, exalting the Father, and being a friend of sinners and investing in a few disciples.

NOTES

Week 1

1. Max Lucado, *Just Like Jesus* (Nashville: W Publishing Group, 1998), 1–2.

Week 2

1. Louis Berkhof, *Systematic Theology* (Grand Rapids: Eerdmans, 1940), 327, quoted by Charles Buntin in his article "The Empty God."

2. Charles Ryrie, *Basic Theology* (Wheaton, Ill.: Victor Books, 1986).

3. Ibid., quoted in Jason Dulle, "Christology" article on apostolic.net/biblicalstudies/christology.htm.

4. Bruce Ware, quoted from a message preached at Christ Community Church in St. Charles, Ill., on November 12, 1996.

5. Wayne Grudem, *Systematic Theology* (Grand Rapids: Zondervan, 1994), 539.

6. For an extended article on this topic, you can go to sonlifeclassic.com and download a free copy of "The Humanity of Jesus" by Dann Spader.

7. Dick Staub, *About You: Fully Human, Fully Alive* (San Francisco: Josey-Bass, 2010), 139.

Week 3

1. Gerald Hawthorne, *The Presence & the Power: The Significance of the Holy Spirit in the Life and Ministry of Jesus* (Eugene, Ore.: Wipf and Stock Publishers, 1991), 99.

Week 4

1. Dann Spader, *Harmony Study*, 12–25. For more information and a listing of these thirty-three different instances and the forty-five verses in which they're found, visit sonlifeclassic.com.

2. Ann Spangler and Lois Tverberg, *Sitting at the Feet of Rabbi Jesus: How the Jewishness of Jesus Can Transform Your Faith* (Grand Rapids: Zondervan, 2000), 45.

Week 5

1. Trading My Sorrows, Words and Music by Darrell Evans, © 1998 Integrity's Hosanna! Music/ASCAP, c/o Integrity Media, Inc., 1000 Cody Road, Mobile, AL 36695. All Rights Reserved. International Copyright Secured. Used by Permission. Reprinted by permission of Hal Leonard Corporation

Week 7

1. Dann Spader and Dave Garda, *33 Things That Happen at the Moment of Salvation*, Sonlife Ministries, 2010. This resource is available at sonlifeclassic.com as a devotional study booklet.

Week 8

1. Robert E. Coleman, *The Master Plan of Evangelism* (Grand Rapids: Revell, 1963), 33.

2. Larry Huntsperger, *The Fisherman* (Grand Rapids: Revell, 2003), 28–29.

3. Ibid., 27–28.

4. Personal interview conducted with Bruce Marchiano in 2000 during a Sonlife Disciplemaking conference. The video is *Matthew, A Dramatic Presentation of the Life of Christ* produced by Thomas Nelson and the Visual Bible, 1999.

5. Eternal CPR is a registered trademark of Sonlife Ministries. Not to be used without permission.

Week 9

1. Developed by Sonlife Ministries and used in the *Disciplemaking from the Life of Christ* manual for their 2:6 Groups (taken from 1 John 2:6). These 2:6 Groups are peer-learning communities designed for leaders to study the life of Christ. For more information visit sonlifeclassic.com.

ACKNOWLEDGMENTS

Walking as Jesus Walked is the result of many lessons learned by various people through the years. While I have developed the core of this study, many have contributed in various ways. My deep respect and appreciation goes to:

- The Leadership Team of Global Youth Initiative; John Abrahamse in Africa, Mark Edwards in Latin America, Bill Hodgson in Australia, Dave Patty in Eastern Europe, and Andrew Tay in Singapore, along with Steve and Don in North America . . . your tireless effort at seeing movements of multiplying disciples in your region of the world has been a great inspiration.
- The board of Sonlife Ministries; Tom Fisher, Scott Krill, Randy Meridith, Jim Rabelhofer, Steve Hudson, and Don Roscoe . . . thanks for hanging with me all these years and making such a difference in your labor of love behind the scenes.
- The faithful prayer supporters and donors of GYI and Sonlife, who keep us out on the front lines of ministry by your sacrificial gifts.
- The hundreds of Sonlife certified trainers and 2:6 Group facilitators who through the years have sacrificially invested in teaching the life of Christ to that next generation . . . as "iron sharpens iron" we continue to learn from each other new aspects of Christ's life. I can't think of anyone I'd rather go off to battle with!
- Special thanks to staff friends who have had such a significant impact on my life . . . Dave and Rennie Garda, Eric Liechty, Bill Clem, Dan and Jean Milliken, Santha Yinger, and the many other staff of Sonlife who through the years partnered in teaching Christ's life to others.
- To the team at Spread Truth who currently works behind the scenes to support Sonlife . . . JD and Amy Bridges, Josh Jeffrey, Amy Horine, and Christine Decker.

- To Dennis Moore who worked so hard to put together the Leader's Guide to help us all be more effective in leading others in this study.
- To Randall Payleitner for his constant encouragement in putting this study together, to Brandon O'Brian and Pam Pugh for their insightful editorial skills, and the rest of the Moody Publishers team who were a joy to work with throughout this process. This would have been impossible without the partnership of Moody.

Since 1979, Sonlife Ministries has trained youth pastors, pastors, and church leaders in disciple-making from the life of Christ. Our passion is simply to create a movement of multiplying disciples committed to living out the character and priorities of Christ. At this time, we are primarily doing this by training leaders in 2:6 Groups (taken from 1 John 2:6). These peer-learning communities are groups of leaders who commit for one to two years of ongoing learning to go deeper in understanding the life of Christ. For more information on this training or for additional resources, you can go to sonlifeclassic.com.

ABOUT THE AUTHOR

Dr. Dann Spader is presently serving as president of Global Youth Initiative. For twenty-five years, Dann served as founder and director of Sonlife Ministries. He has also served for twelve years in a pastoral role in churches. Dann is the father of three daughters, Julie, Jamie, and Christy. He lives in Batavia, Illinois, with his wife, Char.

Dann graduated from Moody Bible Institute in 1975 with a BA degree in Evangelism. He received both a MRE and DMin from Trinity Evangelical Divinity School in Deerfield, Illinois, and has also done graduate work at Wheaton College.

Dann has written twenty leadership-training manuals, is the coauthor of *Growing Healthy Churches*, has contributed several chapters in books, written numerous articles, and produced six training videos. Over 750,000 leaders have been through face-to-face training with material Dann has written on the life of Christ.

Sonlife Ministries develops disciple-making leadership in local churches around the world. It is committed to the training of church leaders in priorities of Great Commission and Great Commandment health as understood in the life of Christ.

The Global Youth Initiative (GYI) is an alliance of more than fifty ministries around the world, which are committed to creating indigenous movements of multiplication with younger leaders. All of these international ministries are involved in advancing the training and values of the Son's life—many of them having grown out of Sonlife Ministries in North America. There are International extensions of Sonlife currently in such diverse areas as Africa, Eastern Europe, Central America, Australia, and the Pacific Rim. The vision of GYI is to see 100,000 proven young leaders raised up . . . multiplying from everywhere to everywhere.

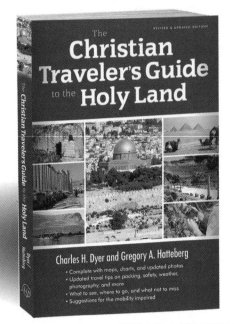

ISBN: 978-0-8024-1162-4

Understand the Bible in New and Vivid Ways

Charles Dyer, a Bible scholar and veteran Holy Land tour guide, and Greg Hatteberg, graduate of the Institute of Holy Land Studies in Jerusalem, created this reference guide for pilgrims who want to deepen the spiritual impact of their trip to Israel, as well as other travelers who just want to know more. Where did Jesus walk? Where is King David buried? Where is Mt. Sinai?

You'll find detailed information about five key Bible lands: Israel, Egypt, Greece, Jordan, and Turkey. This guide includes a full color 32-page photo insert, practical tips for travelers, a 4-week prayer guide for preparing for your trip, detailed maps and an outline of Bible history.

This revised edition features newly excavated sites, up-to-date photos and maps, and relevant advice for preparing for and preserving your trip.

MOODY
PUBLISHERS

www.moodypublishers.com

Sonlife

Muvement
Seminars

A Strategy for **Making** and **Multiplying** Disciples as Jesus did...

Sonlife Ministries conducts leadership seminars called

Muvement:
A Strategy for Making and Multiplying Disciples as Jesus did.

These events can be brought to your church or area and are normally 6-8 hours in length. They cover the 4 Chairs, plus give an overview of how Jesus built a movement of multiplying disciples.

THE SEMINAR INCLUDES TOPICS SUCH AS:
— What is our mission?
— What is our motive?
— Why is Jesus our model?
— What does a disciple look like?
— How did Jesus create a movement of multiplying disciples?

Host or find a seminar near you by visiting our website: Sonlife.com
Each Muvement attendee receives a 75 page training manual and a Sonlife certified trainer.

Sonlife.com

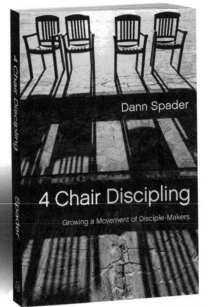

ISBN: 978-0-8024-1207-2

Will your church make disciples?

How does someone go from seeking truth about Jesus to knowing Him and making disciples in His name? Well, it's not easy. But it is simple.

Teacher and leader Dann Spader explains disciple-making as a process of moving people through four chairs, from someone seeking to know more about Christ to someone who makes disciples themselves.

Chair 1: Come and See (John 1:39)
Chair 2: Follow Me (John 1:43)
Chair 3: Become a Fisher of Men (Matthew 4:19)
Chair 4: Go and Bear Fruit (John 15:16)

In the process of His four-year ministry, Jesus recognized that different people are at different stages of growth and development, and He works to challenge each of them to move to the next level.

In *4 Chair Discipling* you'll get a clear and simple picture of how to follow in Jesus' footsteps and do the same thing.

"Of all the disciplers I know, my friend Dann Spader is at the top of the list. He disciples with his life, through his seminars and workshops, and now, thankfully, through this powerful book. Highly recommended!"
Joe Stowell, president of Cornerstone University

MOODY
PUBLISHERS
www.moodypublishers.com